Dedication
To all those who ever struggled with learning a foreign language and to Wolfgang Karfunkel

Copyright © 2024
Yatir Nitzany
All rights reserved.
ISBN-13: 978-1951244750
Printed in the United States of America

Foreword

About Myself

For many years I struggled to learn Spanish, and I still knew no more than about twenty words. Consequently, I was extremely frustrated. One day I stumbled upon this method as I was playing around with word combinations. Suddenly, I came to the realization that every language has a certain core group of words that are most commonly used and, simply by learning them, one could gain the ability to engage in quick and easy conversational Spanish.

I discovered which words those were, and I narrowed them down to three hundred and fifty that, once memorized, one could connect and create one's own sentences. The variations were and are *infinite*! By using this incredibly simple technique, I could converse at a proficient level and speak Spanish. Within a week, I astonished my Spanish-speaking friends with my newfound ability. The next semester I registered at my university for a Spanish language course, and I applied the same principles I had learned in that class (grammar, additional vocabulary, future and past tense, etc.) to those three hundred and fifty words I already had memorized, and immediately I felt as if I had grown wings and learned how to fly.

At the end of the semester, we took a class trip to San José, Costa Rica. I was like a fish in water, while the rest of my classmates were floundering and still struggling to converse. Throughout the following months, I again applied the same principle to other languages—French, Portuguese, Italian, and Arabic, all of which I now speak proficiently, thanks to this very simple technique.

This method is by far the fastest way to master quick and easy conversational language skills. There is no other technique that compares to my concept. It is effective, it worked for me, and it will work for you. Be consistent with my program, and you too will succeed the way I and many, many others have.

Vedat Atacan (MSc) is an independent researcher and linguist. He studied Korean culture and the Korean language at Keimyung University in Daegu. He speaks French, English, Korean, and Italian, and he has 19 publications.

CONVERSATIONAL KOREAN QUICK AND EASY SERIES

The Most Innovative Technique To Learn the Korean Language

PART - 1, PART – 2, PART - 3

YATIR NITZANY

And

VEDAT ATACAN

Check out my website:
www.Conversational-Languages.com

CONTENTS

The Korean Language 8
Memorization Made Easy 10

Korean – I 11
Introduction to the Program 12
The Program 14
Building Bridges 36
Other Useful Tools in the Korean Language 41

Korean – II 43
Introduction to the Program 44
Travel 46
Transportation 50
City 52
Entertainment 54
Foods 57
Vegetables 60
Fruits 62
Shopping 65
Family 68
Human Body 70
Health and Medical 72
Emergencies and Natural Disasters 75
Home 78

Korean – III 83
Introduction to the Program 84
Office 86
School 89
Profession 92
Business 94
Sports 97
Outdoor Activities 99
Electrical Devices 101
Tools 103
Auto 104
Nature 105
Animals 109
Religion, Holidays, and Traditions 112
Wedding and Relationship 115
Politics 117
Military 121

Congratulations, Now You Are On Your Own 125
Note from the Author 127
Also by Yatir Nitzany 128

The Korean Language

The Korean language belongs to the Ural-Altaic language family of Central Asia.

Korea, which initially used Classical Chinese and Chinese letters, changed its written language over time, taking into account the difficulty of the Chinese alphabet and the fact that most of the population was illiterate.

It creates the Korean language called Hangıl.

Korean is the native language for about 80 million people, mostly of Korean descent.

It is the official and national language of both North Korea and South Korea (geographically Korea).

Korean Sentence Structure Patterns

Let's go over the common Korean sentence structure patterns. To start, we need to first be familiar with how basic Korean sentence structures are set up. In an English sentence, the structure is usually Subject, Verb, Object (SVO).

For example, let's look at this English sentence structure that uses subject-verb-object pattern:

I see the cat

Subject – Verb – Object

The sentence structure in Korean is **Subject + Object + Verb**
For example,

- I am **going** to **school** - jeoneun haggyoe gayo
- **I study Korean** - jeoneun hangug-eoleul gongbuhaeyo

In Korean, the subject is the second important element of the sentence after the verb. Since there is no personal suffix in Korean, if the subject is not specified in the sentence, it is not fully understood what the subject is. Therefore, in Korean, the subject is usually found within the sentence. Subject; It can be a noun or case verb group or a word that replaces a noun and takes subject suffixes. The subject suffix changes depending on whether the subject ends in a vowel or a consonant.

Memorization Made Easy

There is no doubt the three hundred and fifty words in my program are the required essentials in order to engage in quick and easy basic conversation in any foreign language. However, some people may experience difficulty in the memorization. For this reason, I created Memorization Made Easy. This memorization technique will make this program so simple and fun that it's unbelievable! I have spread the words over the following twenty pages. Each page contains a vocabulary table of ten to fifteen words. Below every vocabulary box, sentences are composed from the words on the page that you have just studied. This aids greatly in memorization. Once you succeed in memorizing the first page, then proceed to the second page. Upon completion of the second page, go back to the first and review. Then proceed to the third page. After memorizing the third, go back to the first and second and repeat. And so on. As you continue, begin to combine words and create your own sentences in your head. Every time you proceed to the following page, you will notice words from the previous pages will be present in those simple sentences as well, because repetition is one of the most crucial aspects in learning any foreign language. Upon completion of your twenty pages, *congratulations,* you have absorbed the required words and gained a basic, quick-and-easy proficiency and you should now be able to create your own sentences and say anything you wish in the Korean language. This is a crash course in conversational Korean, and it works!

Conversational Korean Quick and Easy
The Most Innovative Technique to Learn the Korean Language

Part I

YATIR NITZANY

And

VEDAT ATACAN

Introduction to the Program

People often dream about learning a foreign language, but usually they never do it. Some feel that they just won't be able to do it while others believe that they don't have the time. Whatever your reason is, it's time to set that aside. With my new method, you will have enough time, and you will not fail. You will actually learn how to speak the fundamentals of the language—fluently in as little as a few days. Of course, you won't speak perfect Korean at first, but you will certainly gain significant proficiency. For example, if you travel to Korea, you will almost effortlessly be able engage in basic conversational communication with the locals in the present tense and you will no longer be intimidated by culture shock. It's time to relax. Learning a language is a valuable skill that connects people of multiple cultures around the world—and you now have the tools to join them.

How does my method work? I have taken twenty-seven of the most commonly used languages in the world and distilled from them the three hundred and fifty most frequently used words in any language. This process took three years of observation and research, and during that time, I determined which words I felt were most important for this method of basic conversational communication. In that time, I chose these words in such a way that they were structurally interrelated and that, when combined, form sentences. Thus, once you succeed in memorizing these words, you will be able to combine these words and form your own sentences. The words are spread over twenty pages. In fact, there are just nine basic words that will effectively build bridges, enabling you to speak in an understandable manner (please see Building

Bridges, page 36). The words will also combine easily in sentences, for example, enabling you to ask simple questions, make basic statements, and obtain a rudimentary understanding of others' communications. I have also created Memorization-Made-Easy Techniques (See page 10) for this program in order to help with the memorization of the vocabulary.

My book is mainly intended for basic present tense vocal communication, meaning anyone can easily use it to "get by" linguistically while visiting a foreign country without learning the entire language. With practice, you will be 100 percent understandable to native speakers, which is your aim. One disclaimer: this is *not* a grammar book, though it does address minute and essential grammar rules. Therefore, understanding complex sentences with obscure words in Korean is beyond the scope of this book.

People who have tried this method have been successful, and by the time you finish this book, you will understand and be understood in basic conversational Korean. This is the best basis to learn not only the Korean language but any language. This is an entirely revolutionary, no-fail concept, and your ability to combine the pieces of the "language puzzle" together will come with *great* ease, especially if you use this program prior to beginning a Korean class.

This is the best program that was ever designed to teach the reader how to become conversational. Other conversational programs will only teach you phrases. But this is the *only* program that will teach you how to create your *own* sentences for the purpose of becoming conversational.

The Program

I / I am na / naneun
With you neowa hamkke
With him / with her geuwa hamkke / geunyeowa hamkke
With us uriwa hamkke
For you dangsin-eul wihae
Without him geueobs-i
Without them geudeul-eobs-i
Always eonjena
Was yeotda
This igeot
Is ida
Sometimes ttaettaero
Maybe amado
Are you dangsin-eun
Better deo na-eun
His / hers geu/geunyeoui geos
He / she geu / geunyeo
From buteo

I am from Korea.
naneun hangug-eseo watseubnida.
Are you from Daegu?
daegueseo osyeossnayo?
I am with you
nanun neowa hamkke
This is for you
igeon neol-wihangeoya
Are you at the house?
jib-e iteoyo?
Sometimes I go without him.
gakkeum naneun geu salam eobs-i gal ttaedo itda.
I am always with her
naneun hangsang geunyeowa hamkke itda
Are you at the house?
jib-e iteoyo?
Sometimes I go without him.
gakkeum naneun geu salam eobs-i gal ttaedo itda.
Are you alone today?
oneul-eun honjayeyo?

I was naneun yeotda
To be ga doeda
The geu
Same gat-eun
Good joh-eun
Here yeogi
It's / it is ida/ida
And geurigo
Between sai
Now jigeum
Later / After najung-e / ihu
If man-yag-e
Yes nae
Then geu da-eum-e
Tomorrow naeil
You neo
Also / too / as well ttohan / neomu / ttohan

I was home at 5pm
naneun ohu 5sie jib-e it-eotda

Between now and tomorrow.
jigeumgwa naeil sai.

It's better to be home later.
najung-e jib-e ganeun geos-i nat-seubnida.

If this is good, then I am happy.
igeos-i johdamyeon jeoneun haengboghabnida.
Yes, you are very good
eung, neon jeongmal chakhae
I was here with them
naneun geudeulgwa hamkke yeogie it-eotda
You and I
neowa na
The same day
gat-eun nal

*This *isn't* a phrase book! The purpose of this book is *solely* to provide you with the tools to create *your own* sentences!

Me na
Ok joh-ayo
Even if birok
Afterwards najung-e
Worse deo nappeun
Where eodi
Everything modeun geot
Somewhere eodinga-e
What mueot
Almost geoui
There geogi
Time sigan
But hajiman
No / not anio / anida
I am not naneun anida
Away tteol-eojyeo
That jeogeot
Similar bisuthan
Other darun
Another tto darun
Day nal
Before jeon-e
Small jag-eun

Where is the airport?
gonghang-i eodi itnayo?

Even if I go now
jigeum gado

Where is everything?
modeun geos-i eodie itseubnikka?

Maybe somewhere
amado eodinga

What? I am almost there
meo? geoui da wat-eo

This is for us.
igeos-eun woorirul wihan geos-ibnida.

House jib
In an-e
Car jadongcha
Already imi
Good morning joh-eun achim-ieyo
How are you? eotteohge jinaeseyo?
Where are you from? eodiseo osyeoynayo?
Today oneul
Hello annyeonghaseyo
What is your name? irum-i mo-eyo?
How old are you? myeot sal-ieyo?
Son adeul
Daughter ttal
At e
Very maeu
Hard ttagttaghan
Still ajig

She is not in the car, so maybe she is still at the house?
geu saram-eun cha an-e eobs-euni ajig jib-e itneun ge anilkkayo?

I am in the car already with your son and daughter
naneun imi dangsin-ui adeulgwa ttalgwa hamkke cha an-e itseubnida

Good morning, how are you today?
joh-eun achim-ieyo, oneul-eun eottaeyo?

Hello, what is your name?
annyeonghaseyo irum-e mueot-ibnikka?

How old are you?
myeot sal-ieyo?

This is very hard, but it's not impossible
igeos-eun maeu aeoryopbjiman bulganeunghajineun anhseubnida

Where are you from?
eodiseo osyeotaeoyo?

*With the knowledge you've gained so far, now try to create your own sentences!

Thank you gamsahabnida
For eul wihan
Anything mueotideun
This is igeos-eun
Time sigan
But hajiman
No / not anio / anida
I am not naneun anida
Away tteol-eojyeo
That jeogeot
Similar bisuthan
Other / Another darun / tto darun
Side yeop
Until kkaji
Yesterday eoje
Without eobs-i
Since buteo
Day nad
For eul wihan
Anything mueotideun
This is igeos-eun

Thank you Kenneth.
gomawoyo kenneth

It's almost time
sigan-i geoui da dwaess-eo

I am not here, I am far away
naneun yeogi eob-go meolli itda

That is a similar house to ours.
uri jibgwa biseushan jib-ineyo.

I am from the other side
naneun bandaepyeon-eseo wat-eoyo

But I was here until late yesterday
geunde na eoje neujgekkaji yeogi it-eoss-eo

Since the other day
jinanbeonbuteo

I say / I am saying jeo/ guronikka
What time is it? jigeum myeot siji?
I want naneun wonhaeyo
Without you neo eobs-ineun
Everywhere /wherever eodiseona/eodiena
I go / I am going naneun ganda / naneun gagoitda
With wa hamkke
My naui
Cousin sachon
I need naneun pil-yohada
Right now jigeum baro
Night bam
To see boda
Light bit
Outside bakk-ui
That is geugeon
Any amugeona
I see / I am seeing naneun bonda / naneun bogo itda
I am saying no naneun aniorago malhagoitda
I say no nan bandae ya

I want to see this during the day
naj-e bogosipda

I see this everywhere
igeon eodiseona bol su it-eo

I am happy without any of my cousins here
yeogie sachon-i eobs-eodo haengbokhaeyo

You need to be at home.
jib-e iss-eoyahabnida.

I see light outside
bakk-e bich-i boyeo

What time is it right now?
jigeum-eun myeotsiibnikka?

Place jangso
Easy swiun
To find chad-da
To look for / to search chad-da / geomsaeghada
Near gakkaun
To wait gidarida
To sell palda
To use sayonghada
To know alda
To decide gyeoljeonghada
Between sai
Two dul
To ege

This place is easy to find
i gos-eun chadgi swibseubnida

I need to look for you next to the car
cha yeop-eseo neorul chaj-aya hae

I am saying to wait until tomorrow
naeilkkaji gidalilago hane

It's easy to sell this table
i teibeul-eun palgi swiwoyo

I want to use this
naneun igeos-eul sayonghago sipda

Where is the book?
geu chaeg-eun eo diyni?

I need to decide between both places
du gos jung hanarul golaya haeyo

I need to know that everything is ok
modeun geos-i gwaenchanhdaneun geos-eul al-aya haeyo

I need to look for you at the mall
syopingmol-eseo dangsin-eul chaj-aya haeyo

Is this place near?
i gos-i geuncheoe itnayo?

Because waenyahamyeon
To buy sada
Both dul da
Them/ They geudeul
Their geudeul-ui
Book chaeg
Mine nae-geot
To understand ihaehada
Problem / Problems munje/munje
I do / I am doing handa/ hago iitda
Of eui
To look boda
Myself nae jasin
Enough chungbunhan
Food eumsig
Water mul
Hotel hotel

I like this hotel because it's near the beach
i hotel-eun haebyeon geuncheoe it-eoseo joh-ayo
I want to look at the view.
geu gwang-gyeong-eul bogo sipseubnida.
I want to buy a bottle of water
mul han byeong-eul sago sip-eoyo
Both of them have enough food
dul da eumsig-i chungbunhaeyo
Do it like this!
ireohge haeboseyo!
That book is mine.
geu chaeg-eun nae geos-ida.
I have to understand the problem
munjerul ihaehaeya haeyo
From the hotel I have a view of the city
hotel-eseo sinaega boyeoyo
I can work today
oneul-eun ilhal su it-eoyo
I do what I want.
naneun naega wonhaneun geos-eul handa.

I like joh-ayo
There is / There are geogieissda
Family / Parents gajog/bumo
Why wae
To say malhada
Something mueos
To go gada
Ready junbi
Soon god
To work ilhada
Who nu-gu
To know alda

I like to be at my house with my parents
naneun bumonimgwa hamkke jib-e itneun geos-eul joh-ahanda

Why do I need to say something important?
wae jung-yohan mal-eul haeya habnikka?

I am there with him
naneun geu saramgwa hamkke it-eoyo

I am busy, but I need to be ready soon
bappeujiman ppalli junbihaeya haeyo

I like to go to work
naneun chulgeunhaneun geos-eul joh-ahanda

Who is there?
geogi nuguya?

I want to know if they are here.
naneun geudeul-i yeogi itneunji algo sipseubnida.

I can go outside.
bakk-e nagal su it-eoyo.

There are seven dolls
jeogi-e inhyeong ilgop-gaega iss-eoyo

How much eolmana manh-i
To bring gajyeooda
With me narang
Instead daesin-e
Only ojig
When eonje
I can / Can I? hal su iss-eoyo / hal su iss-eoyo?
Or ttoneun
Were ieotda
Without me na-eobs-i
Fast pparun
Slow neurin
Cold chuun
Inside naebue
To eat meogda
Hot deoun
To Drive unjeonhada

How much money do I need to bring with me?
eolmana manh-eun don-eul gajigo gaya habnikka?

I like bread instead of rice.
jeoneun babbodaneun ppang-eul joh-ahaeyo.

Only when you can
dangsin-i hal su iss-eul ttaeman

Go there without me.
na eobs-i geogiro gaseyo.

I need to drive the car very fast or very slowly
charul aju pparuge ttoneun aju cheoncheonhi unjeonhaeya haeyo

It is cold inside the library
doseogwan an-eun chuwoyo

I like to eat a hot meal for my lunch
naneun jeomsim-eulo ttatteushan eumsig-eul meogneun geos-eul joh-ahanda

To answer daedabhada
To fly bihaenghada
Today oneul
To travel yeohaenghada
To learn baeuda
How eotteohge
To swim suyeonghada
To practice yeonseubhada
To play nolda
To leave tteonada
Many /much /a lot manhda/manhda/manhda
I go to naneun ganda
First cheot beonjjae
Time / Times sigan / sigan

I need to answer many questions
manh-eun jilmun-e dabhaeya haeyo

The bird must fly
saeneun nal-aya handa

I need to learn to swim at the pool
suyeongjang-eseo suyeonghaneun beob-eul baewoya haeyo

I want to learn how to play better tennis.
naneun teniseurul deo jal chineun bangbeob-eul baeugo sipseubnida.

Everything is about the money.
modeun geos-eun don-e gwanhan geos-ibnida.

I want to leave my dog at home.
gaerul jib-e dugo sip-eoyo.

I want to travel the world.
naneun segyerul yeohaenghago sipda.

Since the first time
cheoeumbuteo

The children are yours
dangsin-eui aideul ibnida

*This *isn't* a phrase book! The purpose of this book is *solely* to provide you with the tools to create *your own* sentences!

Nobody / anyone amudo
Against e majseo
Us woori
To visit bangmunhada
Mom / Mother eom-ma/eomeoni
To give juda
Which eoneu
To meet mannada
Someone nugu
Just danji
To walk geodda
Around yag
Towards jjog-euro
Than boda
Nothing / Anything amugeotdo

Something is better than nothing
amugeotdo eobsneun geotbodaneun mwongaga natda

I am against him
naneun geue bandaehanda

We go to visit my family each week
urineun maeju gajog-eul bangmunhareo gabnida

I need to give you something
dangsin-ege julgeot-i itaeoyo

Do you want to meet someone?
nugungarul mannago sipnayo?

I am here on Wednesdays as well
naneun suyoil-edo yeogi it-eoyo

You do this everyday?
maeil haseyo?

You need to walk around the school.
haggyo jubyeon-eul dol-adanyeoya habnida.

I have naneun gajigoitda
Don't haji anhda
Friend chingu
To borrow billida
To look like cheoleom boida
Grandfather hal-abeoji
To want wonhada
To stay meomuruda
To continue gyesoghada
Way bangbeob
That's why geuleohgi ttaemun-e
To show boyeojuda
I am not going naneun gaji anh-eul geos-ida

Do you want to look like Arnold
Arnoldcheorum boigo sipnayo?

I want to borrow this book for my grandfather
hal-abeojikke i chaeg-eul billyeodeuligo sipseubnida.

I want to drive and to continue on this way to my house
unjeonhaeseo jibkkaji i gil-eul gyesog gago sip-eoyo

I want to stay in Daegu because I have a friend there
daegue chinguga it-eoseo gyesog meomulgo sip-eoyo

I am not going to see anyone here
yeogiseon amudo bol su eobs-eul geoya

I need to show you how to prepare breakfast
achim sigsa junbihaneun bangbeob-eul boyeojwoya haeyo

Why don't you have the book?
wae chaeg-i eobsnayo?

That is incorrect, I don't need the car today
teullyeoss-eoyo. oneul-eun chaga pil-yohaji anh-ayo

To remember gieoghada
Your dangsin-ui
Number sutja
Hour sigan
Dark / darkness eoduun
About e daehan
Grandmother halmeoni
Five daseot
Minute / minutes bun/bun
More deo
To think saeng-gaghada
To do hada
To come kada
To hear deudda
Last majimag

You need to remember my number
nae beonhorul gieoghaeya hae

This is the last hour of darkness
jigeum-eun eodum-ui majimag sigan-ida

I want to come with you.
naneun dangsingwa hamkke gago sipseubnida.

I can hear my grandmother speaking Korean.
halmeoniga hangug-eoro malhaneun soriga deullibnida.

I need to think about this more.
igeos-e daehae deo saeng-gaghae bol pil-yoga it-eoyo.

From here until there, it's only five minutes
yeogiseobuteo geogikkaji dan 5bun

*With the knowledge you've gained so far, now try to create your own sentences!

To leave tteonada
Again dasi
To take gajida
To try sidohada
To rent imdaehada
Without her geunyeoeobs-i
To turn off kkeuda
To ask mudda
To stop geumanhada
Permission heoga

He needs to leave and rent a house at the beach
geuneun tteonaseo haebyeon-e jib-eul billyeoya hae

I want to pass the test without her
geu salam eobs-i siheom-e habgyeoghago sip-eo

We are here a long time
ulineun olaetdong-an yeogie itseubnida

I need to turn off the lights early tonight
oneul bam-eneun bul-eul iljjig kkeoya haeyo

We want to stop here
ulineun yeogiseo meomchugo sipda

We are from Korea.
ulineun hangug-eseo watseubnida.

Your doctor is in the same building.
damdang uisaga gat-eun geonmul-e itseubnida.

In order to leave you have to ask permission.
tteonalyeomyeon heolag-eul bad-aya habnida.

To open yeolda
To buy sada
To pay jibulhada
Last majimag
Without eobs-i
Sister jamae
To hope balada
To live salda
Nice to meet you mannaseo bangawoyo
Name irum
Last name seong
To return dollyeo juda
Enough chungbunhan
Door mun

I need to open the door for my sister
eonnileul wihae mun-eul yeol-eojwoya haeyo

I need to buy something
mwo jom sayaget-eo

I want to meet your brothers.
naneun dangsin-ui hyeongjedeul-eul mannago sipseubnida.

Nice to meet you, what is your name and your last name?
mannaseo bangabseubnida. ileumgwa seong-eun mueos-ibnikka?

We can hope for a better future.
ulineun deo na-eun milaeleul gidaehal su itseubnida.

It is impossible to live without problems.
munjeeobs-i saneun geos-eun bulganeunghabnida.

I want to return to the United States.
naneun migug-eulo dol-agago sipda.

Why are you sad right now?
jigeum wae seulpeungayo?

To happen il-eonada
To order jumunhada
To drink masida
Excuse me sillyehabnida
Child eolin-i
Woman yeoseong
To begin / To start sijaghada
To finish kkeutnaeda
To help dowajuda
To smoke dambaeleul piuda
To love salanghada
To talk / to speak malhada

This must happen today
oneul ileon il-i il-eonaya hae
Excuse me, my child is here as well
joesonghabnida. je aido yeogi it-eoyo
I want to order a soup.
supeuleul jumunhago sip-eoyo.
We want to start the class soon.
ulineun god sueob-eul sijaghago sipseubnida.
In order to finish at three o'clock this afternoon, I need to finish soon
oneul ohu 3sie kkeutnaelyeomyeon ppalli kkeutnaeya haeyo
I want to learn how to speak perfect Korean
naneun wanbyeoghan hangug-eoleul malhaneun beob-eul baeugo sipseubnida.
I don't want to smoke again
dasineun dambaeleul piugo sipji anh-ayo
I want to help
nan dowajugo sip-eoyo
I love you
salanghaeyo
I see you
naneun dangsin-eul bonda
I need you
nan niga pil-yohae

To read ilgda
To write sseuda
To teach galeuchida
To close dad-da
To turn on kkuda
To prefer / to choose seonhohada / seontaeghada
To put nohda
Less deo jeog-eun
Sun hae
Month wol
I talk naega malhada
Exact jeonghwaghan

I need this book to learn how to read and write in Korean.
hangullo ilgo sseuryomyon i chag-i pil-yohaeyo
I want to teach English in Korea.
naneun hangug-eseo yeong-eoleul galeuchigo sipda.

I want turn on the lights and close the door.
bul-eul kyeogo mun-eul dadgo sip-eoyo.

I want to pay less than you.
naneun dangsinboda jeog-eun don-eul jibulhago sipseubnida.

I prefer to put this here.
naneun igeos-eul yeogie duneun geos-eul seonhohabnida.

I speak with the boy and the girl in Korean.
naneun geu sonyeon, sonyeowa hangug-aeolo iyagileul nanunda.

There is sun outside today.
oneul bakk-eneun haega tteunda.

Is it possible to know the exact date?
jeonghwaghan naljjaleul al su itnayo?

*This *isn't* a phrase book! The purpose of this book is *solely* to provide you with the tools to create *your own* sentences!

To exchange bakkuda
To call jeonhwahada
Brother hyeongje
Dad appa
To sit anda
Together hamkke
To change bakkuda
Of course mullon
Welcome hwan-yeong
During dong-an
Years yeonlyeong
Sky haneul
Up wilo
Down alaee
Sorry joesonghabnida
To follow ttaleuda
Her /him geunyeo/geu
Big keun
New saeloun
Never jeoldae

I never want to exchange this money at the bank
nan jeoldae i don-eul eunhaeng-eseo hwanjeonhago sipji anh-a
I want to call my brother and my dad today
oneul-eun hyeong-ilang appahante jeonhwahago sip-eo
Of course I can come to the theater, and I want to sit together with you and with your sister
mullon geugjang-e gal sudo issgo, neowa ne yeodongsaeng-gwa hamkke anjgo sip-eo.
If you look under the table, you can see the new rug.
teibeul alaeleul bomyeon sae leogeuga boibnida.
I can see the sky from the window
changbakk-eulo haneul-i boyeoyo
I am sorry.
mianhaeyo.
The dog wants to follow me to the store.
gaeneun naleul ttala gage-e gago sip-eohabnida.

*With the knowledge you've gained so far, now try to create your own sentences!

To allow heolak-hada
To believe midda
Morning achim
Except je-oehago
To promise yagsoghada
Good night annyeonghi jumuseyo
To recognize insighada
People salamdeul
To move idonghada
Far meol-li
Different daleun
Man namseong
To enter deul-eogada
To receive badda
Good afternoon joh-eun ohuipnida
Through eul tonghae
Him / her geuleul geunyeoleul

I need to allow him to go with us.
geu salam-i uliwa hamkke gal su itdolog heolaghaeya haeyo.
He is a different man now.
geuneun ije daleun salam-i doeeotseubnida.
I believe everything except for this
igeos ppaegoneun da mid-eoyo
Come here quickly.
ppalli yeogilo oseyo.
I must promise to say good night to my parents each night
maeil bam bumonim-ege jal jalago yagsoghaeya haeyo
I can't recognize him.
naneun geuleul al-abol su eobs-seubnida.
I need to move your cat to another chair
ne goyang-ileul daleun uijalo olmgyeoya hae
They want to enter the competition and receive a free book
geudeul-eun daehoee chamgahago mulyo chaeg-eul badgo sip-eohabnida.
I see the sun throughout the morning from the kitchen
naneun achim naenae bueok-eseo taeyang-eul bonda
I go into the house from the front entrance and not through the yard.
madang-eul tonghaji anhgo hyeongwanmun-eulo jib-e deul-eogabnida.

To wish sowon-eul bilda
Bad nappeun
To get eod-da
To forget ijda
Everybody / Everyone modeun salam
Although hajiman
To feel neukkida
Great eomcheongnan
Next da-eum
To like joh-ahada
In front ap-e / **Behind** dwie
Person salam
Well jal
Restaurant sigdang
Bathroom hwajangsil
Goodbye annyeonghi gaseyo

I don't want to wish you anything bad
naneun dangsin-ege nappeun geos-eul giwonhago sipji anhseubnida
I must forget everybody from my past.
gwageoui modeun salam-eul ij-eoya habnida.
I am next to the person behind you
naneun ne dwie issneun salam yeop-e itda
To feel well I must take vitamins
gibun-i joh-ajilyeomyeon bitamin-eul seobchwihaeya haeyo
Goodbye my friend.
annyeong nae chingu.
Which is the best restaurant in the area?
i jiyeog-eseo gajang joh-eun leseutolang-eun eodiingayo?
I can feel the heat.
yeolgiga neukkyeojibnida.
I need to repair a part of the cabinet of the bathroom.
hwajangsil sunabjang ilbuleul sulihaeya haeyo.
She has to get a car before the next year
geunyeoneun naenyeon-i doegi jeon-e chaleul saya hae
I like the house, but it is very small
jib-eun ma-eum-e deuljiman neomu jag-ayo

To remove jegeohada
Please jebal
Beautiful aleumdaun
To lift deulda
Include / Including poham
Belong sok-hada
To hold boyuhada
To check hwag-inhada
Real jinjja
Week ju
Size kugi
Even though iljilado
Doesn't geuleohji anhda
So geulaeseo
Price gagyeog

She wants to remove this door please
geunyeoneun i mun-eul jegeohago sip-eohabnida.
This doesn't belong here, I need to check again
yeogie soghaji anhseubnida. dasi hwag inhaeya habnida.
This week the weather was very beautiful
ibeonjuneun nalssiga neomu joh-at-eoyo
Is that a real diamond?
geugeo jinjja daiamondeu-ingayo?
We need to check the size of the house
jib keugileul hwag-inhaeya haeyo
I want to lift this.
naneun igeos-eul deul-eoolligo sipda.
The sun is high in the sky.
taeyang-i haneul nop-i tteo itseubnida.
Can you please put the wood in the fire?
jangjag-eul bul sog-e neoh-eo jusigess-eoyo?
I can pay this although that the price is expensive
gagyeog-i bissado igeon nael su it-eoyo
Including everything is this price correct?
modeun geos-eul pohamhamyeon i gagyeog-i majnayo?
Can you please hold my hand?
je son-eul jab-a jusigess-eoyo?
I want to go to sleep
naneun jago sipda.

Building Bridges

In Building Bridges, we take six conjugated verbs that have been selected after studies I have conducted for several months in order to determine which verbs are most commonly conjugated. The following three pages contain these six conjugated verbs in first, second, third, fourth, and fifth person, as well as some sample sentences. Please master the entire program up until *here* prior to venturing onto this section.

I want naneun wonhada
I need naneun pil-yohada
I can naneun hal su it-eoyo
I like naneun joh-ayo
I go naneun ganda
I have naneun gajigoitda
I have to / I must naneun haeya handa

I want to go to my house
uli jib-e gago sipda

I can go with you to the bus station
beoseu jeonglyujangkkaji neowa hamkke gal su it-eo

I need to leave the museum.
bagmulgwan-eul tteonaya haeyo.

I like to eat oranges.
naneun olenjileul meogneun geos-eul joh-ahabnida.

I am going to teach a class
sueob-eul halyeogo haeyo

I have to speak to my teacher
seonsaengnimkke yaegihaeya haeyo

You want / do you want?
dangsin-eun wonhaeyo / dangsin-eun wonhaeyo?
He wants / does he want?
geuga wonhaeyo / wonhaeyo?
She wants / does she want?
geunyeoneun wonhaeyo / wonhaeyo?
We want / do we want?
ulineun wonhaeyo / wonhaeyo?
They want / do they want?
geudeul-eun wonhabnikka / geudeul-eun wonhabnikka?
You (plural) want?
yeoleobun-eun wonhasibnikka?

You need / do you need?
pil-yohaeyo / pil-yohaeyo?
He needs / does he need?
geu salam-i pil-yohaeyo / geu salam-i pil-yohaeyo?
She needs / does she need?
geunyeoneun pil-yohaeyo / pil-yohaeyo?
We want / do we want?
ulineun wonhaeyo / wonhaeyo?
They need / do they need?
geudeul-eun pil-yohabnikka / pil-yohabnikka?
You (plural) need
dangsin-eun pil-yo

You can / can you
Dangsin-eun hal su it-eoyo / hal su it-eoyo?
He can / can he
geuneun hal su it-eoyo / geuneun hal su itdeoyo?
She can / can she
geunyeoneun hal su iteoyo/ geunyeoneun hal su iteoyo?
We can / can we?
ulineun hal su it-eoyo / hal su itnayo?
They can / can they?
geudeul-eun hal su irnayo? / geuleol su irnayo?
You (plural) can?
dangsin-eun hal su irseubnikka?

You like / do you like?
joh-ahaeyo / joh-ahaeyo?
He likes / does he like?
geu salam-i joh-ahaeyo / joh-ahaeyo?
She like / does she like?
geunyeoneun joh-ahaeyo / joh-ahaeyo?
We like / do we like?
ulineun joh-ahaeyo / joh-ahaeyo?
They like / do they like?
geudeul-eun joh-ahaeyo / joh-ahaeyo?
You (plural) like?
dangsin-eun joh-ahabnikka?

You go / do you go?
gaseyo / gasinayo?
He goes / does he go?
geu salam gayo / gaseyo?
She goes / does she go?
geunyeoneun gayo / gaseyo?
We go / do we go?
ulineun gayo / uli gayo?
They go / do they go?
geudeul-eun gayp / gayo?
You (plural) go?
dangsin-eun gaseyo?

You have / do you have?
dangsin-eun it-eoyo / it-eoyo?
He has / does he have?
geu salam-eun it-eoyo / it-eoyo?
She has / does she have?
geunyeoneun gajigo it-eoyo / gajigo it-eoyo?
We have / do we have?
uliegen it-eoyo / it-eoyo?
They have / do they have?
geudeul-eun gajigo it-eoyo / gajigo itnayo?
You (plural) have?
dangsin-eun gajigo itnayo?

Do you want to go?
dangsin-eun gago sipji anhseubnida?

Does he want to fly?
geuneun nalgo sip-eohabnikka?

We want to swim
ulineun suyeonghago sip-eo

Do they want to run?
geudeul-eun dalligo sip-eohabnikka?

Do you need to clean?
Cheongsohaeya habnikka?

She needs to sing a song
geunyeoneun nolaeleul bulleoya hae

We need to travel
ulineun yeohaeng-eul haeya haeyo

They don't need to fight
geudeul-eun ssaul pil-yoga eobs-seubnida

You (plural) need to save your money.
dangsin-eun don-eul jeochughaeya habnida.

Can you listen to me?
nae mal jom deul-eojullae?

He can dance very well
geuneun chum-eul aju jal chunda

We can go out tonight
uli oneul bam-e nagal su iss-eo

The fireman can break the door during an emergency.
sobang-gwan-eun bisangsi mun-eul busul su itseubnida.

Do you like to eat here?
yeogiseo meogneun geol joh-ahasinayo?

He likes to spend time here
geuneun yeogiseo sigan-eul bonaeneun geol joh-ahaeyo

We like to fix the house
ulineun jib-eul gochineun geol joh-ahaeyo

They like to cook
geudeul-eun yolihaneun geos-eul joh-ahanda

You (plural) like to play soccer.
dangsin-eun chugguhaneun geos-eul joh-ahaeyo.

Do you go to the movies on weekends?
jumal-e yeonghwaboleo gasinayo?

He goes fishing
geuneun nakksihaleo ganda

We are going to relax
ulineun hyusig-eul chwihal yejeong-ida

They go out to eat at a restaurant every day.
geudeul-eun maeil sigdang-e nagaseo sigsaleul habnida.

Do you have money?
don-iss-eo?

She must look outside
geunyeoneun bakk-eul bwaya hae

We have to sign our names
uli ileum-eulo seomyeonghaeya hae

They have to send the letter
geudeul-eun pyeonjileul bonaeya hae

You (plural) have to stand in line.
dangsin eun jul-eul seoya habnida.

OTHER USEFUL TOOLS FOR THE KOREAN LANGUAGE

Days of the Week yo-il
Sunday il-yoil
Monday wol-yoil
Tuesday hwa-yoil
Wednesday su-yoil
Thursday mog-yoil
Friday geum-yoil
Saturday to-yoil

Seasons gyejeol
Spring bom / **Summer** yeoleum
Autumn ga-eul / **Winter** gyeoul

Cardinal Directions gyeoul
North bugjjog / **South** namjjog
East dongbu / **West** seojjog

Numbers sutja
One hana
Two dul
Three set
Four net
Five dasod
Six yeosod
Seven ilgob
Eight yodol
Nine ahob
Ten yol

Colors saek-kkal
White hayansaeg
Gray hoesaeg
Yellow nolansaeg
Green nogsaeg
Orange juhwangsaeg
Purple bolasaeg
Brown galsaeg
Red ppalgansaeg
Blue palansaeg
Black geom-eunsaeg

Conclusion

Congratulations! You have completed all the tools needed to master the Korean language, and I hope that this has been a valuable learning experience. Now you have sufficient communication skills to be confident enough to embark on a visit to Korea, impress your friends, and boost your resume so *good luck*.

This program is available in other languages as well, and it is my fervent hope that my language learning programs will be used for good, enabling people from all corners of the globe and from all cultures and religions to be able to communicate harmoniously. After memorizing the required three hundred and fifty words, please perform a daily five-minute exercise by creating sentences in your head using these words. This simple exercise will help you grasp conversational communications even more effectively. Also, once you memorize the vocabulary on each page, follow it by using a notecard to cover the words you have just memorized and test yourself and follow *that* by going back and using this same notecard technique on the pages you studied during the previous days. This repetition technique will assist you in mastering these words in order to provide you with the tools to create your own sentences.

Every day, use this notecard technique on the words that you have just studied.

Everything in life has a catch. The catch here is just consistency. If you just open the book, and after the first few pages of studying the program, you put it down, then you will not gain anything. However, if you consistently dedicate a half hour daily to studying, as well as reviewing what you have learned from previous days, then you will quickly realize why this method is the most effective technique ever created to become conversational in a foreign language. My technique works! For anyone who doubts this technique, all I can say is that it has worked for me and hundreds of others.

Conversational Korean Quick and Easy

The Most Innovative Technique to Learn the Korean Language

Part II

YATIR NITZANY

And

VEDAT ATACAN

Introduction to the Program

In the first book, you were taught the 350 most useful words in the Korean language, which, once memorized, could be combined in order for you to create your own sentences. Now, with the knowledge you have gained, you can use those words in Conversational Korean Quick and Easy Part 2 and Part 3, in order to supplement the 350 words that you've already memorized. This combination of words and sentences will help you master the language to even greater proficiency and quicker than with other courses.

The books that comprise Parts 2 and 3 have progressed from just vocabulary and are now split into various categories that are useful in our everyday lives. These categories range from travel to food to school and work, and other similarly broad subjects. In contrast to various other methods, the topics that are covered also contain parts of vocabulary that are not often broached, such as the military, politics, and religion. With these more unusual topics for learning conversational languages, the student can learn quicker and easier. This method is flawless and it has proven itself time and time again.

If you decide to travel Korea, then this book will help you speak the Korean language.

This method has worked for me and thousands of others. It surpasses any other language-learning method system currently on the market today.

This book, Part 2, specifically deals with practical aspects concerning travel, camping, transportation, city living, entertainment such as films, food including vegetables and fruit, shopping, family including grandparents, in-laws, and stepchildren, human anatomy, health, emergencies, and natural disasters, and home situations.

The sentences within each category can help you get by in other countries.

In relation to travel, for example, you are given sentences about food, airport necessities such as immigration, and passports. Helpful phrases include, "Where is the immigration and passport control inside the airport?" and "I want to order a bowl of cereal and toast with jelly." For flights there are informative combinations such as, "There is a long line of passengers in the terminal because of the delay on the runway." When arriving in another country options for what to say include, "We want to hire a driver for the tour. However, we want to pay with a credit card instead of cash" and, "On which street is the car-rental agency?

When discussing entertainment in another country and in a new language, you are provided with sentences and vocabulary that will help you interact with others. You can discuss art galleries and watching foreign films. For example, you may need to say to friends, "I need subtitles if I watch a foreign film" and, 'The mystery-suspense genre films are usually good movies'. You can talk about your own filming experience in front of the camera.

The selection of topics in this book is much wider than in ordinary courses. By including social issue such as incarceration, it will help you to engage with more people who speak the language you are learning.

Part 3 will deal with vocabulary and sentences relevant to indoor matters such as school and the office, but also a variety of professions and sports.

Travel - Yeohaenghada

Flight bihaeng
Airplane bihaeng-gi
Airport gonghang
Terminal teominal
Passport yeogwon / **Customs** segwan
Take off (airplane) ilyughada
Landing (airplane) chaglyug
Departure chulbal / **Arrival** dochag
Gate mun
Luggage suhwamul / **Suitcase** yeohaeng-gabang
Baggage claim suhamul chajneun
Passenger (Male) seung-gaeg / **Passenger** (Female) seung-gaeg

I like to travel.
naneun yeohaeng-eul joh-ahabnida.
This is a very expensive flight.
igeos-eun maeu bissan bihaeng-ibnida.
The airplane takes off in the morning and lands at night.
bihaeng-gineun achim-e ilyughaeseo bam-e chaglyughabnida.
My suitcase is at the baggage claim.
nae yeohaeng-gabang-eun suhamul chajneun gos-e it-eoyo.
We need to go to the departure gate instead of the arrival gate.
dochag geiteuga anin chulbal geiteulo gaya habnida.
There is a long line of passengers in the terminal because of the delay on the runway.
hwaljulo jiyeon-eulo inhae teomineol-eneun seung-gaegdeul-ui jul-i gilge neul-eoseo itseubnida.
What is your final destination?
dangsin-ui choejong mogjeogjineun mueos-ibnikka?
I don't like to sit above the wing of the airplane.
naneun bihaeng-gi nalgae wie anjneun geol joh-ahaji anhneunda.
The flight takes off at 3pm, but the boarding commences at 2:20pm.
bihaeng-gineun ohu 3sie ilyughajiman tabseung-eun ohu 2si 20bunbuteo sijagdoebnida.
Do I need to check in my luggage?
suhamul-eul chekeu-inhaeya hanayo?
Where is the passport control inside the airport?
gonghang nae yeogwon simsadaeneun eodie itnayo?
I am almost finished at customs.
segwan tong-gwaga geoui kkeutnatseubnida.

International flight gugjeseon / **Domestic flight** gugnaeseon
First class ildung-seok / **Business class** bizness-seok
Economy class ikonomi-seok
Round trip wangbog yeohaeng / **One-way flight** pyeondo bihaeng
Return flight gwigugpyeon / **Direct flight** jighangpyeon
Flight attendant seungmuwon
Layover / connection hwanseung / hwanseung
Reservation yeyag
Security check boan geomsa
Checked bags witagsuhamul / **Carry on bag** ginae suhwamul
Business trip chuljang
Check in counter chekeu-in kaunteo
Travel agency yeohaengsa
Temporary visa imsi bija / **Permanent visa** yeong-gu bija
Country nara

The flight attendant told me to go to the check in counter.
seungmuwon-i chekeu-in kaunteolo galago haess-eoyo.
For international flights, you must be at the airport three hours before the flight.
gugjeseon-ui gyeong-u bihaeng 3sigan jeonkkaji gonghang-e dochaghaeya habnida.
For a domestic flight, I need to arrive at the airport at least two hours before the flight.
gugnaeseon-ui gyeong-u bihaeng-gi chulbal choeso 2sigan jeonkkaji gonghang-e dochaghaeya habnida.
Business class is usually cheaper than first class.
bijeuniseu keullaeseuneun ilbanjeog-eulo ildung keullaeseuboda jeolyeomhabnida.
I purchased my plane tickets at the travel agency.
yeohaengsa-eseo bihaeng-gipyoleul gumaehaet-eoyo.
The one-way ticket is cheaper than the round-trip ticket.
pyeondo tikes-eun wangbog tikesboda jeolyeomhabnida.
I prefer a direct flight without a layover.
naneun hwanseung eobs-i jighang hang-gongpyeon-eul seonhohabnida.
I must make reservations for my return flight.
dol-aoneun hang-gongpyeon-eul yeyaghaeya haeyo.
Why do I need to remove my shoes at the security check?
boan geomsaegdaeeseo sinbal-eul beos-eoya haneun iyuneun mueos-ibnikka?
I have three checked bags and one carry-on.
witagsuhamul 3gaewa ginaesuhamul 1gaega itseubnida.
I have to ask my travel agent if this country requires an entry visa.
i nala-e ibgug bijaga pil-yohanji yeohaengsa-e mun-uihaeya habnida.

Trip yeohaeng
Tourist gwangwang-gaeg / **Tourism** gwangwang
Holiday hyuil/ **Vacations** hyuga
Currency exchange Hwanjeon
Port of entry ibgughang
Car rental agency lenteoka daelijeom
Identification Sinbunjeong
GPS nebigeisyeon / **Map** jido
Road dolo
Information center inpomaesionsenteo
Bank eunhaeng
Hotel hotel
Leisure yeoga
Driver unjeonsa
Tour gwangwang
Credit sin-yong cad / **Cash** hyeongeum
A travel guide yeohaeng gaideu
Ski resort seuki lijoteu

I had an amazing trip.
naneun nollaun yeohaeng-eul haessda.
The currency exchange counter is past the port of entry.
hwanjeonsoneun ibgughang-eul jinaseo itseubnida.
There is a lot of tourism during the holidays and vacations.
yeonhyuna hyugacheol-eneun gwangwang-i manh-i bumbibnida.
Where is the car-rental agency?
lenteoka hoesaneun eodie itnayo?
You need to show your identification whenever checking in at a hotel.
hotel-e chekeu-inhal ttaemada sinbunjeung-eul jesihaeya habnida.
It's more convenient to use the GPS on the roads instead of a map.
dolo-eseoneun jido daesin GPSleul iyonghaneun geos-i deo pyeonlihabnida.
Why is the information center closed today?
oneul jeongbosenteoneun wae mun-eul dadnayo?
When I am in a new country, I go to the bank before I go to the hotel.
jeoneun saeloun nala-e iss-eul ttae hotel-e gagi jeon-e eunhaeng-e gabnida.
I need to book my leisure vacation at the ski resort today.
oneul-eun seukijang-eseo yeoga hyugaleul yeyaghaeya haeyo.
We want to hire a driver for the tour.
tueoe unjeongisaleul goyonghago sipseubnida.
We want to pay with a credit card instead of cash.
hyeongeum daesin sin-yongkadeulo gyeoljehago sipseubnida.
Does the tour include an English-speaking guide?
tueoe yeong-eo gaideuga pohamdoeeo itnayo?

Transportation – unsong

Car jadongcha
Bus beoseu / **School bus** haggyo beoseu
Station yeog
Train gicha / **Train station** gichayeog / **Train tracks** gicha teulaeg
Subway jihacheol
Taxi taegsi
Motorcycle otobai / **Scooter** seukuteo
Helicopter hellikobteo
Limousine limujin
Driver license unjeon myeonheojeung
Vehicle registration chalyang deunglog / **License plate** beonhopan
Ticket tikes / **Ticket (penalty)** beomchig-gum

Where is the public transportation?
daejung-gyotong-eun eodie itnayo?
Where can I buy a bus ticket?
beoseupyoneun eodiseo sal su istnayo?
Please call a taxi.
taegsileul bulleojuseyo.
In some cities, you don't need a car because you can rely on the subway.
ilbu dosieseoneun jihacheol-eul iyonghal su itgi ttaemun-e jadongchaga pilyohaji anhseubnida.
Where is the train station?
gichayeog-eun eodie itnayo?
The train cart is still stuck on the tracks.
gicha suleneun yeojeonhi seonlo-e but-eo itseubnida.
The motorcycles make loud noises.
otobaineun keun solileul naenda.
Where can I rent a scooter?
seukuteoneun eodieseo billil su itnayo?
I want to schedule a helicopter tour.
hellikobteo tueoleul yeyaghago sip-eoyo.
I want to go to the party in a limousine.
limujin-eul tago patie gago sip-eoyo.
Don't forget to bring your driver's license and registration.
unjeonmyeonheojeung-gwa deunglogjeung-eul jichamhaneun geos-eul ij-ji maseyo.
The cop gave me a ticket because my license plate is expired.
nae beonhopan-i manlyodoeeossgi ttaemun-e gyeongchal-i na-ege ttagjileul jwotseubnida.

Truck teuleog
Pickup truck pig-eob teuleog
Bicycle jajeongeo
Van bong-gocha
Gas station juyuso
Gasoline gasollin
Tire taieo
Oil change enjin oil gyohwan
Tire change taieo gyoche
Mechanic jeongbigong
Canoe kanu
Ship bae / **Boat** boteu
Yacht yoteu / **Sailboat** yoteu
Motorboat moteoboteu
Marina jeongbak-ji / **A dock** budu
Cruise keulujeu / **Cruise ship** yulamseon
Ferry peri
Submarine jamsuham

I can put my bicycle in my truck.
nae teuleog-e jajeongeoleul sil-eul su iss-eoyo.
Where is the gas station?
juyusoneun eodie itnayo?
I need gasoline and also to put air in my tires.
hwibal-yudo pil-yohago taieoe gong-gido neoh-eoya habnida.
I need to take my car to the mechanic for a tire and oil change.
taieowa oil-eul gyochehalyeomyeon jeongbiso-e chaleul gajyeogaya habnida. **I can bring my canoe in the van.**
kanuleul baen-e sil-eul su it-eoyo.
Can I bring my yacht to the boat show at the marina?
seonchagjang-eseo yeollineun boteu syoe yoteuleul gajyeool su itnayo?
I prefer a motorboat instead of a sailboat.
naneun beomseonbodaneun moteoboteuleul deo joh-ahanda.
I want to leave my boat at the dock on the island
baeleul seom-ui seonchagjang-e dugo sip-eoyo
This spot is a popular stopping point for the cruise ship.
i jijeom-eun yulamseon-ui ingi itneun jeongcha jijeom-ibnida.
This was an incredible cruise.
igeos-eun nollaun keulujeuyeotseubnida.
Do you have the schedule for the ferry?
peli iljeong-i itnayo?
The submarine is yellow.
jamsuham-eun nolansaeg-ida.

City – dosi

Village ma-eul
House jib
Home jib
Apartment apateu
Tower - taweo
Building geonmul
Neighborhood iut
Office building samusil geonmul
Post office uchegug
Location wichi
Elevator ellibeiteo / **Stairs** gyedan
Fence ultali
Construction site geonseolhyeonjang
Bridge dali
Gate mun
City hall sicheong
The mayor sijang
Fire department sobang-seo
Fireman sobang-gwan

Is this a city or a village?
igeos-eun dosiinga, ma-eul-inga?
Does he live in a house or an apartment?
geuneun jib-ina apateue salgo itnayo?
This residential building does not have an elevator, just stairs.
i jugeoyong geonmul-eneun ellibeiteoga eobsgo gyedanman itseubnida.
These skyscrapers are located in the new part of the city.
i gocheung bilding-eun dosiui saeloun jiyeog-e wichihae itseubnida.
The tower is tall but the building beside it is very short.
tab-eun nopjiman geu yeop geonmul-eun maeu jjalbseubnida.
This is a historical neighborhood.
igos-eun yeogsajeog-in dongneibnida.
There is a fence around the construction site.
gongsajang jubyeon-eneun ultaliga chyeojyeo itseubnida.
The post office is located in that office building.
uchegug-eun geu samusil geonmul-e itseubnida.
The bridge is closed today.
oneul dalineun pyeswaedoeeotsseubnida.
The gate is open.
mun-i yeollyeo itseubnida.
The fire department is located in the building next to city hall.
sobangseoneun sicheong yeop geonmul-e itseubnida.

Street geoli / **Main street** keungil / **Sidewalk** bodo
Parking jucha / **To park** juchahada / **Parking lot** juchajang
Traffic gyotong /**Traffic light** sinhodeung / **Red light** ppalganbul
Yellow light nolanbul/ **Green light** chologbul
Toll lane yulyo chaseon
Fast lane ppaleun chaseon /**Slow lane** neulin chaseon
Left lane oenjjog chaseon / **Right lane** oleunjjog chaseon
Highway gosogdolo / **Intersection** gyochalo / **Tunnel** teoneol
U-turn yuteon / **Shortcut** jileumgil
Stop sign jeongji sinho /**Pedestrians** bohaengja
Crosswalk hoengdan bodo

Parking is on the main street and not on the sidewalk.
juchaneun bodoga anin mein seuteuliteue itseubnida.
Where is the parking lot?
juchajang-eun eodie itnayo?
The traffic is very bad today.
oneul-eun gyotong-i maeu nappeubnida.
You must avoid the fast lane because it's a toll lane.
gosogchaloneun yulyochaloimeulo pihaeya habnida.
I don't like to drive on the highway.
naneun gosogdolo-eseo unjeonhaneun geos-eul joh-ahaji anhseubnida.
At a red light you need to stop, at a yellow light you must be prepared to stop and at a green you can drive.
ppalgan sinhodeung-eseoneun jeongjihaeya hago, nolansaeg sinhodeung-eseoneun jeongjihal junbileul haeya hamyeo, nogsaeg sinhodeung-eseoneun unjeonhal su itseubnida.
This road has too many traffic lights.
i gil-eneun sinhodeung-i neomu manh-ayo.
At the intersection, you need to stay in the right lane instead of the left lane because that's a bus lane.
gyochalo-eseoneun oenjjog chaseon-i anin oleunjjog chaseon-i beoseu jeonyong chaseon-imeulo, oleunjjog chaseon-eulo juhaenghaeya habnida.
The tunnel seems longer than yesterday.
teoneol-i eojeboda gil-eojin geos gat-ayo.
This is a short drive.
jjalb-eun unjeon geoliibnida.
The next bus stop is far away.
da-eum beoseu jeonglyujang-eun meolli itseubnida.
You need to turn right at the stop sign and then continue on straight.
jeongji sinho-eseo uhoejeonhan hu gyesog jigjinhaeya habnida.
Pedestrians use the crosswalk to cross the road.
bohaengjaneun gil-eul geonneogi wihae hoengdanbodoleul iyonghabnida.

Capital sudo
Resort lijoteu
Port poteu
Road dolo
Trail jaguk
Bus station beoseu jeonglyujang / **Bus stop** beoseu jeonglyujang
Night club naiteu keulleob
Downtown dosim
District guyeog
County gun
Statue dongsang
Monument ginyeommul
Castle seong
Cathedral seongdang
Zoo dongmul-won
Science museum gwahag bagmulgwan
Playground nol-i-teo
Swimming pool suyeongjang
Jail gyodoso

The capital is a major attraction point for tourists.
sudoneun gwangwang-gaegdeul-ege juyo maelyeog pointeu-ibnida.
The resort is next to the port.
lijoteuneun hang-gu yeop-e itseubnida.
The night club is located in the downtown district.
naiteukeulleob-eun sinae jiyeog-e wichihae itseubnida.
This statue is a city monument.
i dongsang-eun dosi ginyeommul-ibnida.
This is an ancient castle.
igeos-eun godae seong-ibnida.
That is a beautiful cathedral.
jeongmal aleumdaun daeseongdang-ineyo.
Do you want to go to the zoo or the science museum?
dongmul-won-e gago sipnayo, animyeon gwahaggwan-e gago sipnayo?
The children are in the playground.
aideul-eun nol-iteoe it-eoyo.
The swimming pool is closed for the community today.
suyeongjang-eun oneul jiyeog sahoeleul wihae pyeswaedoeeotseubnida.
You need to follow the trail alongside the main street to reach the bus station. beoseu jeonglyujang-e galyeomyeon mein seuteuliteuleul ttala sanchaegloleul ttalagaya habnida.
The jail in this county is very small.
i kauntiui gam-og-eun maeu jagseubnida.

Entertainment – olag

Movie yeonghwa
Theater (movie theater) geugjang /yeonghwagwan
Actor baeu / **Actress** yeobaeu
Genre jangleu
Subtitles jamag
Action aek-syeon
Foreign oegug-ui
Mystery sinbi
Suspense seosupensu
Documentary dakyumenteori/ **Biography** jeongi
Drama deulama
Comedy komedi
Romance lomaenseu
Horror gongpo
Animation aenimaeisyeon/ **Cartoon** manhwa
Director gamdog / **Producer** jaejak-ja/ **Audience** cheongjung

There are three new movies at the theater that I want to see.
geugjang-e bogo sip-eun sae yeonghwaga se pyeon it-eoyo.
He is a really good actor.
geuneun jeongmal joh-eun baeu-ibnida.
She is an excellent actress.
geunyeoneun hullyunghan yeobaeu-ibnida.
That was a good action movie.
joh-eun aegsyeon-yeonghwayeossseubnida.
I need subtitles if I watch a foreign film.
oegug-yeonghwaleul bolyeomyeon jamag-i pil-yohaeyo.
Films of the mystery-suspense genre are usually good movies.
miseuteoli seoseupenseu jangleuui yeonghwaneun daegae joh-eun yeonghwaibnida.
I like documentary films. However, comedy-drama or romance films are better.
naneun dakyumenteoli yeonghwaleul joh-ahanda. hajiman komidi deulamana lomaenseu yeonghwaga deo johseubnida.
Sometimes biographies are boring to watch.
ttaeloneun jeongileul boneun geos-i jiluhal ttaedo itseubnida.
My favorite genre of movies are the horror movies.
jega gajang joh-ahaneun yeonghwa jangleuneun gongpoyeonghwaibnida.
It's fun to watch animated movies.
aenimeisyeon yeonghwaleul boneun geos-eun jaemiitseubnida.
The director and the producer can meet the audience today.
oneul gamdoggwa peulodyuseoga gwangaegdeul-eul mannal su itda.

Television tellebijeon
A show (as in television) syo
A show (as in live performance) syo
Channel chaeneol
Series silijeu / **Episode** hwa
Commercial gwang-go
Anchorman aengkeomaen / **Anchorwoman** aengkeoumeon
News sosig / **News station** nyuseu seuteisyeon
Screening sang-yeong
Live laibu / **Broadcast** bangsong
Headlines hedeulain
Viewer sichung-ja
Speech yeonseol
Script daebon
Screen hwamyeon / **Camera** kamela

It's already time to buy a new television.
ije sae tellebijeon-eul gu-ibhal sigan-i doeeotseubnida.
This was the first episode of this television show yet it was a long series.
igeos-eun i TV syoui cheos beonjjae episodeuyeossjiman gin silijeuyeotseubnida.
There aren't any commercials on this channel.
i chaeneol-eneun gwang-goga eobs-seubnida.
This anchorman and anchorwoman work for our local news station.
i aengkeomaengwa yeoseong aengkeomaen-eun uli jiyeog nyuseu bangsong-gug-eseo ilhabnida.
They decided to screen a live broadcast on the news.
geudeul-eun nyuseuleul saengbangsong-eulo sang-yeonghagilo gyeoljeonghaetseubnida.
The news station featured the headlines before the program began.
nyuseu bangsong-gug-eseoneun peulogeulaem-i sijagdoegi jeon-e hedeulain-eul jangsighaetseubnida.
Tonight, all the details about the incident were mentioned on the news.
oneul bam, nyuseueseoneun sageon-e daehan modeun sebusahang-i eongeubdoeeotseubnida.
The viewers wanted to hear the presidential speech today.
sicheongjadeul-eun oneul daetonglyeong yeonseol-eul deudgo sip-eohaetseubnida.
I must read my script in front of the screen and the camera
seukeulingwa kamela ap-eseo daebon-eul ilg-eoya haeyo.
We want to enjoy the entertainment tonight.
ulineun oneul bam olag-eul jeulgigo sipseubnida.

Theater (play) geugjang
A musical myujikeol
A play yeon-guk
Theater stage geugjang mudae
Audition odisyeon
Performance gong-yeon
Box office bagseu opiseu
Ticket pyo
Singer gasu
Band baendeu
Orchestra okeseuteula / **Opera** opela
Music eum-ag
Song nolae
Musical instrument aggi / **Drum** deu-lum
Guitar gita / **Piano** piano
Trumpet teuleompes
Violin baiollin / **Flute** peulluteu
Art misul
Gallery gaelleoli
Studio studio
Museum bagmulgwan

It was a great musical performance.
hullyunghan myujikeol gong-yeon-ieotseubnida.
Can I audition for the play on this stage?
i mudaeeseo yeongeug odisyeon-eul bol su itnayo?
She is the lead singer of the band.
geunyeoneun baendeuui lideu sing-eoida.
I will go to the box office tomorrow to purchase tickets for the opera.
naneun naeil maepyoso-e gaseo opela pyoleul sal geos-ida.
The orchestra needs to perform below the stage.
okeseuteulaneun mudae alaeeseo yeonjuhaeya habnida.
I like to listen to this type of music.
naneun ileon jonglyuui eum-ag-eul deudneun geos-eul joh-ahabnida.
I hope to hear a good song.
joh-eun nolae deullyeojusyeoss-eumyeon johgetseubnida.
The common musical instruments that are used in a concert are drums, guitars, pianos, trumpets, violins, and flutes.
konseoteue sayongdoeneun ilbanjeog-in aggiloneun deuleom, gita, piano, teuleompes, baiollin, peulluteu deung-i itseubnida.
The art gallery has a studio for rent.
misulgwan-eneun imdae seutyudioga itseubnida.
I went to an art museum yesterday.
naneun eoje misulgwan-e gatda.

Foods – sigpum

Grocery store siglyopumjeom
Market sijang
Supermarket syupeomakes
Groceries sig-pum
Butcher shop jeong-yuk jeom / **Butcher** - jeong-yuk jeom juin
Bakery ppangjib / **Baker** jaeppang-sa
Breakfast achim / **Lunch** jeomsim / **Diner** jeo-neok
Meat gogi / **Chicken** dak
Seafood haemul
Egg gyelan
Milk uyu / **Cheese** chijeu / **Butter** beoteo
Bread ppang / **Flour** milgalu
Oil gileum
Baked guun geos
Cake keikeu
Beer maegju / **Wine** wain
Cinnamon gyepigalu / **Powder** galu
Mustard meoseutadeu

Where is the nearest grocery store?
ajang gakkaun siglyopumjeom-i eodie itaeoyo?
Where can I buy meat and chicken?
gogiwa dalg-gogineun eodiseo sal su itaeoyo?
I need to buy flour, eggs, milk, butter, and oil to bake my cake.
keikeuleul guulyeomyeon milgalu, gyelan, uyu, beoteo, gileum-eul saya haeyo.
The groceries are already in the car.
siglyopum-eun imi cha-e it-eoyo.
Where can I buy beer and wine.
maegjuwa wain-eun eodiseo sal su itaeoyo?
On which aisle is the cinnamon powder?
gyepigaluneun eoneu tonglo-e itaeoyo?
The butcher shop is near the bakery.
jeong-yugjeom-eun ppangjib geuncheoe it-eoyo.
I have to go to the market, to buy a half kilo of meat.
gogi ban gun salyeomyeon sijang-e gaya haeyo.
For lunch, we can eat seafood, and then pasta for dinner.
jeomsim-eneun haesanmul-eul meoggo, jeonyeog-eneun paseutaleul meogseubnida.
I usually eat bread with cheese for breakfast.
jeoneun julo achim-e chijeuwa hamkke ppang-eul meogseubnida.
I don't have any ketchup or mustard to put on my hotdog.
hasdogeue neoh-eul kecheob-ina meoseuteodeuga eobs-eoyo.

Menu menyu
Steak seuteikeu
Hamburger haembeogeo
Water mul
Salad saelleodeu
Soup gug
Beef sogogi / **Lamb** yang-gogi / **Pork** dwaejigogi / **Fish** mulgogi
Appetizer gansig / **Entrée** bonsig
Cooked yoli / **Raw** nalgeos-ui
Boiled salm-eun geos / **Fried** tui-gin geos / **Grilled** guun geos
Dessert dijeoteu
Ice cream aiseukeulim
Olive oil ollibeuyu
Juice juseu
Coffee keopi / **Tea** cha
Honey kkul / **Sugar** seoltang

Do you have a menu in Korean?
hangug-eolo doen menyuga itaeoyo?
Which is preferable, the fried fish or the grilled lamb?
saengseontwigimgwa yang-gogi gu-i jung eoneu geos-i deo johnayo?
I want to order a cup of water, a soup for my appetizer, and pizza for my entrée.
mul han keob, jeonchae yolilo supeu, mein menyulo pijaleul jumunhago sipseubnida.
I want to order a steak for myself, a hamburger for my son, and ice cream for my wife.
naneun nae jasin-eul wihae seuteikeuleul jumunhago, nae adeul-eul wihae haembeogeoleul, nae anaeleul wihae aiseukeulim-eul jumunhago sipseubnida.
Which type of dessert is included with my coffee?
nae keopieneun eotteon jonglyuui dijeoteuga pohamdoeeo itaeoyo?
Can I order a salad with a hard boiled egg and olive oil on the side?
salm-eun dalgyalgwa ollibeu oil-eul gyeotdeul-in saelleodeuleul jumunhal su itaeoyo?
Is the piece of fish in the sushi cooked or raw?
chobab-e deul-eoganeun saengseon jogag-eun jolidoen geos-ingayo animyeon nalgeos-ingayo?
I want to order a fruit juice instead of a soda.
tansan-eumlyo daesin gwail juseuleul jumunhago sip-eoyo.
I want to order tea with a teaspoon of honey instead of sugar.
seoltang daesin kkul han tiseupun-eul neoh-eun chaleul jumunhago sip-eoyo.
The tip is 20% at this restaurant.
i sig-dang-ui tib-eun 20%ibnida.

Vegetarian chaesigjuuija / **Vegan** bigeon
Dairy nagnong / **Dairy products** yujepum
Salt sogeum / **Pepper** huchu / **Sauce** - Sauce soseu
Flavor mat / **Spices** hyanglyo
Rice ssal / **Fries** twigim
Soy ganjang
Nuts gyeongwalyu / **Peanuts** ttangkong
Sandwich saendeuwichi
Mayonnaise mayonejeu
Chocolate chokollis /**Cookies** kuki /**Candy** satang
Jelly jelli / **Whipped cream** hwiping keulim
Popsicle eol-umgwaja
Frozen aeol-lin / **Thawed** haedongdoem

I don't eat meat because I am a vegetarian.
naneun chaesigjuuijaigi ttaemun-e gogileul meogji anhneunda.
My brother won't eat dairy products because he is a vegan.
nae dongsaeng-eun chaesigjuuijaigi ttaemun-e yujepum-eul meogji anh-eul geoyeyo.
Food tastes much better with salt, pepper, and spices.
sogeum, huchu, hyangsinlyoleul sayonghamyeon eumsig-ui mas-i hwolssin joh-ajibnida.
The only things I have in my freezer are popsicles.
nae naengdongsil-e issneun geon aiseukaendippun-ieyo.
No chocolate, candy, or whipped cream until after dinner.
jeonyeog sigsaga kkeutnal ttaekkaji chokollis, satang, hwipingkeulim-eun geumjidoebnida.
I want to try a sample of that piece of cheese.
geu chijeu saempeul-eul meog-eobogo sip-eoyo.
I have allergies to nuts and peanuts.
naneun gyeongwalyuwa ttangkong-e alleleugiga itseubnida.
This sauce is disgusting.
i soseuneun yeoggyeowoyo.
Why do you always put mayonnaise on your sandwich?
saendeuwichie wae hangsang mayonejeuleul neoh-eoyo?
The food is still frozen so we need to wait for it to thaw.
eumsig-i ajig naengdongdoeeo iss-eoseo haedongdoel ttaekkaji gidalyeoya habnida.
Please bring me a bowl of cereal and a slice of toasted bread with jelly.
silieol han geuleusgwa jellileul gyeotdeul-in guun ppang han jogag-eul gajyeodajuseyo.
It's healthier to eat rice instead of fries.
gamjatwigim daesin bab-eul meogneun geos-i deo geonganghaeyo.

Vegetables – chaeso

Vegetables chaeso
Grilled vegetables guun yachae
Steamed vegetables jjin yachae
Tomato tomato / **Carrot** dang-geun / **Lettuce** sangchu
Radish mu / **Beet** geun-dae
Eggplant gaji
Bell Pepper pimang / **Hot pepper** maeun gochu
Celery selleoli
Spinach sigeumchi
Cabbage yangbaechu / **Cauliflower** kollipeullawo
Beans kong
Corn ogsusu
Garlic maneul / **Onion** yangpa
Artichoke atichokeu

Grilled vegetables or steamed vegetables are popular side dishes at restaurants.
guun yachaena jjin yachaeneun sigdang-eseo ingi itneun banchan-ida.
I put carrots, bell peppers, lettuce, and radishes in my salad.
saelleodeueneun dang-geun, pimang, yangsangchu, muleul neoh-eoyo.
It's not hard to grow tomatoes.
tomato kiugi eolyeobji anh-ayo.
Eggplant can be cooked or fried.
gajineun ik-higeona twigil su itseubnida.
I like beets in my salad.
naneun saelleodeue geun-daeleul neohneun geol joh-ahaeyo.
Why are chili peppers so spicy?
gochuneun wae ileohge maeulkkayo?
Celery and spinach have natural vitamins.
selleoliwa sigeumchieneun cheon-yeon bitamin-i deul-eo itseubnida.
Fried cauliflower tastes better than fried cabbage.
twigin yangbaechuboda twigin kollipeullawoga deo mas-it-eoyo.
Rice and beans are my favorite side dish.
babgwa kong-eun jega jeil joh-ahaneun banchan-ieyo.
I like to put butter on corn.
naneun ogsusue beoteoleul baleuneun geol joh-ahaeyo.
Garlic is an important ingredient in many cuisines.
maneul-eun manh-eun yolieseo jung-yohan seongbun-ibnida.
Where is the onion powder?
yangpagaluneun eodie itaeoyo?
Artichokes are difficult to peel.
atichokeuneun kkeobjil-eul beosgigiga eol yeobseubnida.

Cucumber oi
Lentils lentil kong
Peas wandukong
Herbs heobeu
Basil bajil / **Cilantro** gosu / **Green onion** pa
Dill dil / **Parsley** paseulli / **Mint** minteu
Potato gamja / **Sweet Potato** goguma
Mushroom beoseot
Asparagus aseupalageoseu
Seaweed mi-yeok
Pumpkin hobag / **Squash** hobag
Chick peas byeong-alikong
Vegetable garden chaesobat

I want to order lentil soup.
lenjeukong supeuleul jumunhago sip-eoyo.
Please put the green onion in the refrigerator.
daepaleul naengjang-go-e neoh-eojuseyo.
The most common kitchen herbs are basil, cilantro, dill, parsley, and mint.
gajang heunhan jubang heobeuneun bajil, gosu, dil, paseulli, minteu-ibnida.
Some of the most common vegetables for tempura are sweet potatoes and mushrooms.
twigim-e gajang heunhan yachaeloneun gogumawa beoseot-i itseubnida.
I want to order vegetarian sushi with asparagus and cucumber along with a side of seaweed salad.
aseupalageoseuwa oiga deul-eogan chaesig seusiwa hamkke haecho saelleodeuleul jumunhago sipseubnida.
I enjoy eating pumpkin seeds as a snack.
naneun hobagssileul gansig-eulo jeulgyeo meogseubnida.
I must water my vegetable garden.
chaesobat-e mul-eul jueoya haeyo.
The potatoes in the field are ready to harvest.
bat-e issneun gamjaneun suhwaghal junbiga doeeo itseubnida.
Chickpeas are a popular ingredient in Middle Eastern food.
byeong-alikong-eun jungdong eumsig-eseo ingi itneun jaelyoibnida.
Is there Zucchini in the soup?
supeue hobag-i deul-eoissnayo?
I like to put ginger dressing on my salad.
naneun saelleodeue saeng-gang deulesing-eul neohneun geos-eul joh-ahabnida.
The tomatoes are fresh but the cucumbers are rotten.
tomatoneun sinseonhajiman oineun sseog-eotseubnida.

Fruits – gwail

Apple sagwa / **Banana** banana
Orange olenji / **Grapefruit** jamong
Peach bogsung-a
Tropical fruit yeoldae gwail
Papaya papaya
Coconut kokoneos
Cherry cheli
Raisins geonpodo / **Prunes** seoyang jadu
Dates naljja / **Figs** muhwagwa
Fruit salad gwail saelleodeu / **Dried fruit** mallin gwail
Apricot salgu
Avocado abokado
Ripe ig-eun

Can I add raisins to the apple pie?
sagwa paie geonpodoleul chugahaedo doenayo?
Orange juice is a wonderful source of Vitamin C.
olenji juseuneun bitamin Cui hullyunghan gong-geub-won-ibnida.
Grapefruits are extremely beneficial for your health.
jamong-eun geongang-e maeu yuighabnida.
I have a peach tree in my front yard. nae
apmadang-eneun bogsung-anamuga it-eoyo.
I bought papayas and coconuts at the supermarket to prepare a tropical fruit salad.
yeoldae gwail saelleodeuleul junbihagi wihae syupeomakes-eseo papayawa kokoneos-eul satseubnida.
I want to travel to Japan to see the famous cherry blossom.
naneun yumyeonghan beojkkoch-eul boleo ilbon-e yeohaeng-eul gago sipda.
Bananas are tropical fruits.
banananeun yeoldae gwail-ibnida.
I want to mix dates and figs in my fruit salad.
gwail saelleodeue daechuwa muhwagwaleul seokkgo sip-eoyo.
Apricots and prunes are my favorite dried fruits.
salguwa jaduneun jega gajang joh-ahaneun gwail-ibnida.
Pears are delicious.
baeneun mas-it-eoyo.
The avocados aren't ripe yet.
abokadoneun ajig deol ig-eot-eoyo.
The green apple is very sour.
nogsaeg sagwaneun maeu sikeumhabnida.
The unripe peach is usually bitter.
deol ig-eun bogsung-aneun daegae sseun mas-i nabnida.

Fruit tree gwail namu
Citrus gamgyul
Lemon lemon
Lime laim
Pineapple pain-aepeul
Grapes podo
Pomegranate seoglyu
Plum jadu
Olive ollibeu
Grove sup

Strawberries grow during the Spring.
ttalgineun bom-e jalabnida.
How much does the watermelon juice cost?
subagjuseu gagyeog-eun eolmaingayo?
I have a pineapple plant inside a pot.
hwabun an-e pain-aepeul sigmul-i it-eoyo.
Melons grow on the ground.
mellon-eun ttang-eseo jalabnida.
I am going to the fruit-tree section of the nursery today to purchase a few citrus trees.
naneun oneul gamgyulnamu myeoch geululeul saleo myomogjang gwailnamu koneoe gal yejeong-ibnida.
Pomegranate juice contains a very high level of antioxidants.
seoglyu juseueneun maeu nop-eun sujun-ui hangsanhwajega ham-yudoeeo itseubnida.
I need to pick the grapes to make the wine.
wain-eul mandeullyeomyeon podoleul ttaya haeyo.
How much does the watermelon juice cost?
subagjuseu gagyeog-eun eolmaingayo?
I have a pineapple plant inside a pot.
hwabun an-e pain-aepeul sigmul-i it-eoyo.

Melon mellon
Watermelon subag
Strawberry ttalgi
Berry mallin ssias
Raspberry santtalgi
Blueberry beullubeli

There are many raspberries growing on the bush.
deombul-eneun manh-eun lajeubeliga jalago itseubnida.
Blueberry juice is very sweet.
beullubeli juseuneun maeu dalkomhabnida.
Berries are acidic fruits.
belineun sanseong gwail-ibnida.
Melons grow on the ground.
mellon-eun ttang-eseo jalabnida.
I am going to the fruit-tree section of the nursery today to purchase a few citrus trees.
naneun oneul gamgyulnamu myeoch geululeul saleo myomogjang gwailnamu koneoe gal yejeong-ibnida.
There are many raspberries growing on the bush.
deombul-eneun manh-eun lajeubeliga jalago itseubnida.
Blueberry juice is very sweet.
beullubeli juseuneun maeu dalkomhabnida.
Berries are acidic fruits.
belineun sanseong gwail-ibnida.
Pomegranate juice contains a very high level of antioxidants.
seoglyu juseueneun maeu nop-eun sujun-ui hangsanhwajega ham-yudoeeo itseubnida.
I need to pick the grapes to make the wine.
wain-eul mandeullyeomyeon podoleul ttaya haeyo.
Plums are seasonal fruits.
jaduneun jecheol gwail-ida.
I want to add either lemon juice or lime juice to my salad.
saelleodeue lemonjuseuna laimjuseuleul chugahago sip-eoyo.
I have an olive grove in my backyard.
nae dwismadang-e ollibeu gwasuwon-i it-eoyo.

Shopping – syoping

Clothes ot
Clothing store otgage
For sale hal-in
Hat moja
Shirt syeocheu
Shoes sinbal
Skirt chima / **Dress** deuleseu
Pants baji / **Shorts** banbaji
Suit jeongjang / **Vest** jokki / **Tie** nek-tail
Uniform jebog
Belt belteu / **Socks** yangmal / **Gloves** jang-gab
Glasses angyeong / **Sunglasses** sunglass
Size keugi / **Small** jag-eun / **Medium** jung-gan / **Large** keun
Thick dukkeoun / **Thin** yalb-eun
Thrift store jung-gopum gage

There are a lot of clothes for sale today.
oneul-eun os-i manh-i pallineyo.
Does this hat look good?
i moja gwaenchanh-a boinayo?
I am happy with this shirt and these shoes.
naneun i syeocheuwa i sinbal-i ma-eum-e deubnida.
She prefers a skirt instead of a dress.
geunyeoneun deuleseuboda seukeoteuleul deo joh-ahanda.
These pants aren't my size.
i bajineun nae saijeuga aniya.
Where can I find a thrift store?
jung-gopum gageneun eodieseo chaj-eul su itnayo?
I want to buy a suit, a vest, and a tie.
yangbog, jokki, negtaileul sago sip-eoyo.
There are uniforms for school at the clothing store.
otgagee haggyo gyobog-i it-eoyo.
I forgot my socks, belt, and shorts at your house.
yangmal, belteu, banbajileul dangsin jib-e dugowat-eoyo.
These gloves are a size too small.
i jang-gab-eun keugiga neomu jagseubnida.
Do you have a medium size?
jung-gan saijeuga itnayo?
Today I don't need my reading glasses.
oneul-eun dodbogiga pil-yohaji anhseubnida.
I only need my sunglasses.
seongeullaseuman it-eumyeon doebnida.

Jacket jaekis
Scarf seukapeu / **Mittens** jang-gab
Sleeve somae
Boots (rain, winter) bucheu
Sweater seuweteo
Bathing suit suyeongbog
Flip flops jjo-ri/ **Sandals** saendeul
Tank top - minsomae
Heels hil
On sale halin panmae
Expensive gbissan / **Free** mulyo
Discount hal-in / **Cheap** ssan
Shopping syoping
Mall syoping senteo

We are going to the mountain today so don't forget your jacket, mittens, and scarf.
ulineun oneul san-e gal teni jaekis, beong-eoli jang-gab, seukapeuleul ij-ji maseyo.
I have long sleeve shirts and short sleeve shirts.
ginpal syeocheuwa banpal syeocheuga it-eoyo.
Boots and sweaters are meant for winter.
bucheuwa seuweteoneun gyeoul-yong-ibnida.
At the beach, I wear a bathing suit and flip flops.
haebyeon-eseoneun suyeongboggwa sjjo-rirul sinseubnida.
I want to buy a tank top for summer.
yeoleum-yong minsomae-rul sago sip-eoyo.
I can't wear heels on the beach, only sandals.
haebyeon-eseoneun hil-eul sin-eul su eobsgo saendeulman sin-eul su it-eoyo.
What will be on sale tomorrow?
naeil-eun mueos-eul panmaehal yejeong-ingayo?
This is free.
igeos-eun mulyoibnida.
Even though these colognes and perfumes are discounted, they are still very expensive.
i hyangsuwa hyangsuneun hal-in-eul bad-ass-eum-edo bulguhago yeojeonhi maeu bissabnida.
These items are very cheap.
i pummogdeul-eun maeu jeolyeomhabnida.
I can go shopping only on weekends.
jumal-eman syopinghal su it-eoyo.
Is the local mall far?
dongne syopingmol-i meongayo?

Store gage
Business hours -yeong-up sigan
Open open/ **Closed** dad-eum
Entrance ibgu / **Exit** chulgu
Shopping basket syoping baguni / **Shopping bag** syopingbaeg
Toy store jangnangam gage / **Toy** jangnangam
Book store seojeom / **Music store** eumban gage
Jeweler boseog segong-in / **Jewelry** boseoglyu
Gold geum / **Silver** eun
Diamond daiamondeu / **Necklace** moggeol-i
Bracelet paljji / **Earrings** gwigeol-i
Gift seonmul
Coin dongjeon
Antique goldong-pum/ **Dealer** sang-in

What are your (plural) business hours?
gwihaui yeong-eobsigan-eun eotteohge doebnikka?
What time does the store open?
gageneun myeoch sie yeol-eoyo?
What time does the store close?
gageneun myeoch sie mun-eul dadnayo?
Where is the entrance?
ibguneun eodiingayo?
Where is the exit?
chulguneun eodiibnikka?
My children want to go to the toy store so they can fill up the shopping cart with toys.
uli aideul-eun jangnangam gagee gaseo jangbagunie jangnangam-eul gadeug chaeugo sip-eo habnida.
I need a large shopping basket when I go to the supermarket.
syupeomakes-e gal ttae keun jangbaguniga pil-yohaeyo.
There is a sale at the bookstore right now.
jigeum seojeom-eseo seil jung-ieyo.
It's difficult to find a music store these days.
yojeum-eun eumbanmaejang-eul chajgiga eolyeobseubnida.
The jeweler sells gold and silver.
boseogsang-eseoneun geumgwa eun-eul panmaehabnida.
I want to buy a diamond necklace.
daiamondeu moggeol-ileul sago sip-eoyo.
This bracelet and those pair of earrings are gifts for my daughter.
i paljjiwa jeo gwigeol-ineun nae ttal-eul wihan seonmul-ieyo.
He is an antique coin dealer.
geuneun goldongpum dongjeon sang-in-ibnida.

Family – gajog

Mother eomeoni
Father abeoji
Son adeul
Daughter ttal
Brother hyeong/oppa
Sister nana/un-ni
Husband nampyeon
Wife bu-in
Parents bumo
Child eolin-i
Baby agi
Grandparents jobumo
Grandfather hal-abeoji
Grandmother halmeoni
Grandson sonja
Granddaughter sonnyeo
Grandchildren sonja
Nephew joka / **Niece** joka
Cousin sachon

I have a big family.
uli gajog-eun daegajog-ibnida.
My brother and sister are here.
nae hyeongjewa jamaega yeogie itseubnida.
The mother and father want to spend time with their child.
eommawa appaneun aiwa hamkke sigan-eul bonaego sip-eohabnida.
He wants to bring his son and daughter.
geuneun adeulgwa ttal-eul delyeoogo sip-eohabnida.
The grandfather wants to take his grandson to the movie.
hal-abeojineun sonjaleul yeonghwagwan-e delyeogago sip-eohabnida.
The grandmother needs to give her granddaughter money.
halmeonineun sonnyeoege don-eul jueoyahabnida.
The grandparents want to spend time with their grandchildren.
jobumonim-eun sonjudeulgwa hamkke sigan-eul bonaego sip-eohabnida.
The husband and wife have a new baby.
nampyeongwa anaeegeneun saeloun agiga itseubnida.
I want to go to the park with my niece and nephew.
jokawa hamkke gong-won-e gago sip-eoyo.
My cousin wants to see his children.
nae sachon-i geuui aideul-eul bogo sip-eohaeyo.
That man is a good parent.
geu salam-eun joh-eun bumoyeyo.

Aunt imo / **Uncle** samchon
Man namja / **Woman** yeoja
Stepfather gyebu / **Stepmother** gyemo
Stepson uibut-adeul / **Stepdaughter** uibut-ttal
Stepbrother ibog hyeongje / **Stepsister** ibog nu-i
Half brother iboghyeongje / **Half sister** ibog yeodongsaeng
Ancestor seonjo / **Family tree** gagyedo / **Generation** sedae
Relative chin-chug/ **Family member** gajog guseong-won
First born -ma-ji/ **Only child** oedong
Relative chin-chug
Twins ssangdung-i
Pregnant imsin
Adopted ib-yang-a
Orphan goa
Adult seong-in
Neighbor iut
Friend chingu
Roommate lummeiteu

My aunt and uncle came to visit.
imowa samchon-i bangmunhaetseubnida.
He is their only child.
geuneun geudeul-ui yuilhan janyeoibnida.
My wife is pregnant with twins.
je anaeneun ssangdung-ileul imsinhaet-eoyo.
He is their eldest son.
geuneun geudeul-ui jangnam-ibnida.
The first-born child usually takes on all the responsibilities.
ilbanjeog-eulo cheotjjae aiga modeun chaeg-im-eul matseubnida.
I was able to find all my relatives and ancestors on my family tree.
naneun nae gagyedo-eseo modeun chincheoggwa josang-eul chaj-eul su it-eotseubnida.
My parents' generation loved disco music.
uli bumonim sedaeneun diseuko eum-ag-eul joh-ahaet-eoyo.
Their adopted child was an orphan.
geudeul-ui ib-yang-aneun goayeotseubnida.
I have a nice neighbor.
na-egen joh-eun ius-i itda.
We need to choose a godfather for the baby.
ulineun agiui daebuleul seontaeghaeya habnida.
She considers her stepson as her real son.
geunyeoneun uibus-adeul-eul jinjja adeullo yeogibnida.
She is his stepdaughter.
geunyeoneun geuui uibusttal-ibnida.

Human Body - ingan-ui mom

Head meoli
Face eolgul
Eye nun
Ear gwi
Nose ko
Mouth ib / **Lips** ibsul
Tongue hyeo
Cheek bol
Chin teog
Neck mog / **Throat** mog-gu-mung
Forehead ima
Eyebrow nunsseob / **Eyelashes** sognunsseob
Hair meolikalag
Beard suyeom / **Mustache** kot-suyeom
Tooth ippal

My chin, cheeks, mouth, lips, and eyes are all part of my face.
teog, bol, ib, ibsul, nun modu nae eolgul-ui ilbu-ibnida.
He has small ears.
geuneun gwiga jagseubnida.
I have a cold so my nose, eyes, mouth, and tongue are affected.
gamgie geollyeoseo ko, nun, ib, hyeoga yeonghyang-eul badseubnida.
The five senses are sight, touch, taste, smell, and hearing.
ogam-eun sigag, choggag, migag, hugag, cheong-gag-ibnida.
I am washing my face right now.
naneun jigeum sesuleul hago itda.
I have a headache.
dutong-i it-eoyo.
My eyebrows are too long.
nunsseob-i neomu gil-eoyo.
He must shave his beard and mustache.
geuneun teogsuyeomgwa kot-suyeom-eul myeondohaeya habnida.
I brush my teeth every morning.
naneun maeil achim ileul dakkneunda.
She puts makeup on her cheeks and lipstick on her lips.
geunyeoneun bol-eneun hwajang-eul hago ibsul-eneun libseutig-eul baleunda.
Her hair covered her forehead.
geunyeoui meolikalag-eun imaleul deop-eotseubnida.
he has a long neck.
geuneun mog-i gil-eoyo.
I have a sore throat.
mog-i apeuda.

Shoulder eokkae
Chest gaseum
Arm pal / **Hand** son / **Palm (of hand)** sonbadag
Elbow palkkumchi / **Wrist** sonmog
Finger songalag / **Thumb** muji
Back –dung/heolie
Belly bae / **Stomach** wi / **Intestines** jang
Brain noe
Heart sim-jang
Lungs pye
Kidneys sinjang
Liver gan
Leg dali / **Ankle** balmog / **Foot** bal / **Toe** balgalag
Nail sontop
Joint gwanjeol / **Muscle** geun-yug
Bone ppyeo / **Spine** cheogchu / **Ribs** galbi-ppyeo
Skeleton haegol / **Skull** dugaegol
Skin pibu / **Vein** jeongmaeg

He has a problem with his stomach.
geuneun wijang-e munjega itseubnida.
The brain, heart, kidneys, lungs, and liver are internal organs.
noe, simjang, sinjang, pye, gan-eun naebu jang-giibnida.
His chest and shoulders are very muscular.
geuui gaseumgwa eokkaeneun maeu geun-yugjil-ida.
I need to strengthen my arms and legs.
palgwa dalileul ganghwahaeya haeyo.
I accidentally hit his wrist with my elbow.
silsulo palkkumchilo geuui sonmog-eul chyeot-eoyo.
I have pain in every part of my body especially in my hand, ankle, and back.
mom-ui modeun buwi, teughi son, balmog, heolie tongjeung-i itseubnida.
I want to cut my nails.
sontob-eul jaleugo sip-eoyo.
I need a new bandage for my thumb.
eomjisongalag-e sae bungdaega pil-yohaeyo.
I have a cast on my foot because of a broken bone.
ppyeoga buleojyeoseo bal-e gibseuleul haetseubnida.
I have muscles and joint pain today.
oneul-eun geun-yugtong-gwa gwanjeoltong-i itseubnida.
The spine is the main part of the body.
cheogchuneun sinche-ui juyo bubun-ibnida.
I have beautiful skin.
naneun aleumdaun pibuleul gajigo itseubnida.

Health and Medical – geongang-gwa uilyo

Health geongang
Medical uilyo
Disease jilbyeong / **Bacteria** bagtelia
Sick apeun
Clinic jinlyoso
Headache dutong / **Earache** gwialh-i
Pharmacy yaggug / **Prescription** cheobang
Symptoms jeungsang
Nausea meseukkeoum / **Stomachache** bogtong
Allergy alleleugi
Penicillin penisillin / **Antibiotic** hangsaeng muljil
Sore throat mog sseulim / **Fever** bal-yeol / **Flu** gam-gi
Cough gichim / **To cough** gichimhada
Infection jeon-yeombyeong
Injury busang / **Scar** hyungteo
Ache apeum / **Pain** tongjeung
Intensive care jibjung chilyo
Band-Aid banchang-go / **Bandage** bungdae

Are you in good health?
dangsin-eun geonganghabnikka?
These bacteria caused this disease.
i bagteliaga i jilbyeong-eul il-eukyeotseubnida.
He is very sick.
geuneun maeu apeuda.
I have a headache so I must go to the pharmacy to refill my prescription.
dutong-i it-eoseo yaggug-e gaseo cheobangjeon-eul dasi jojehaeya habnida.
The main symptoms of food poisoning are nausea and stomach ache.
sigjungdog-ui juyo jeungsang-eun meseukkeoumgwa bogtong-ibnida.
I have an allergy to penicillin, so I need another antibiotic.
jeoneun penisillin-e alleleugiga it-eoseo daleun hangsaengjega pil-yohabnida.
What do I need to treat an earache?
gwitongjeung-eul chilyohalyeomyeon mueos-i pil-yohabnikka?
I need to go to the clinic for my fever and sore throat.
yeol-i nago mog-i apaseo byeong-won-e gaya haeyo.
The bandage won't help your infection.
bungdaeneun gam-yeom-e doum-i doeji anhseubnida.
I have a serious injury so I must go to intensive care.
busang-i simhaeseo junghwanjasil-e gaya haeyo.
I have muscle and joint pains today.
yojeum geun-yugtong-gwa gwanjeoltong-i it-eoyo.

Hospital byeong-won
Doctor uisa / **Nurse** ganhosa
Family Doctor juchi-eui / **Pediatrician** soagwa uisa
Medication yagmul / **Pills** alyak
Heartburn sogsseulim
Paramedic eui-ryowon / **Emergency room** eung-geubsil
Health geongang / **Patient** hwan-ja
Surgery susul / **Surgeon** oegwa uisa
Anesthesia machwi
Local anesthesia gugso machwi / **General anesthesia** jeonsin machwi
A walker bohaeng-gi / **A cane** jipang-i
Wheelchair hwill-chae-a / **Stretcher** deulgeot
Dialysis tuseog / **Insulin** insyullin / **Diabetes** dangnyobyeong
Temperature ondo / **Thermometer** ondogye
A shot syat / **Needle** baneul / **Syringe** jusagi

Where is the closest hospital?
gajang gakkaun byeong-won-eun eodiingayo?
Usually we see the nurse before the doctor.
botong ulineun uisaboda ganhosaleul meonjeo bobnida.
The paramedics can take her to the emergency room but she doesn't have health insurance.
gugeubdaewon-i geunyeoleul eung-geubsillo delyeogal su itjiman geunyeoneun geongang boheom-i eobs-seubnida.
The doctor treated the patient.
uisaga hwanjaleul chilyohaetseubnida.
He needs knee surgery today.
geuneun oneul muleup susul-i pil-yohaeyo.
The surgeon needs to administer general anesthesia in order to operate on the patient.
oegwa uisaneun hwanjaleul susulhagi wihae jeonsin machwileul sihaenghaeya habnida.
Does the patient need a wheelchair or a stretcher?
hwanja-ege hwilcheeona deulgeot-i pil-yohabnikka?
I have to take medicine every day.
maeil yag-eul meog-eoya haeyo.
Do you have any pills for heartburn?
sog sseulim-e meogneun yag-i itnayo?
Where is the closest dialysis center?
gajang gakkaun tuseogsenteoneun eodie itnayo?
The doctor didn't prescribe insulin for my diabetes.
uisaneun nae dangnyobyeong-e insyullin-eul cheobanghaji anh-atseubnida.
I need a thermometer to take my temperature.
che-on-eul jaelyeomyeon ondogyega pil-yohaeyo.

Stroke noejoljung
Blood pi / **Blood pressure** hyeol-ab
Heart attack simjangmabi / **Cancer** am / **Chemotherapy** hwahag-yobeob
To help dob-da
Germs segyun / **Virus** baileoseu
Vaccine baegsin / **A cure** chilyo / **To cure** chilyohada
Cholesterol kolleseutelol
Nutrition yeong-yangmul seobchwi / **Diet** daieoteu
Blind nun-i meon / **Deaf** cheong-gag jang-aein / **Mute** Muet
Young eolin / **Elderly** yeonsega deusin
Fat (person) ttungttunghan / **Skinny (person)** malun
Nursing home yoyang-won
Disability – jang-ae/ **Handicap** haendikaeb / **Paralysis** mabi
Depression uuljeung / **Anxiety** bul-an
Dentist chigwa uisa
X-ray egseulei
Tooth cavity chung-chi/ **Tooth paste** chiyag / **Tooth brush** chis-sol

A stroke is caused by a lack of blood flow to the brain.
noejoljung-eun noelo ganeun hyeollyuga bujoghayeo balsaenghabnida.
These are the symptoms of a heart attack.
igeos-i simjangmabiui jeungsang-ibnida.
Chemotherapy is for treating cancer.
hwahag-yobeob-eun am-eul chilyohagi wihan geos-ibnida.
Proper nutrition is very important and you must avoid foods that are high in cholesterol.
jeogjeolhan yeong-yang seobchwiga maeu jung-yohamyeo kolleseutelol hamlyang-i nop-eun eumsig-eul pihaeya habnida.
I am starting my diet today.
oneulbuteo daieoteuleul sijaghagetseubnida.
There is no cure for this virus, only a vaccine.
i baileoseuneun chilyobeob-eun eobsgo baegsinman itda.
The nursing home is open 365 days a year.
yoyang-won-eun 365il yeonjungmuhyulo un-yeongdoebnida.
I don't like suffering from depression and anxiety.
naneun uuljeung-gwa bul-an-eulo gotongbadneun geos-eul joh-ahaji anhseubnida.
Soap and water kill germs.
binuwa mul-eun segyun-eul jug-ibnida.
The dentist took X-rays of my teeth to check for cavities.
chigwa uisaneun chungchileul hwag-inhagi wihae nae chiaui egseuleileul jjig-eotseubnida.
In the morning I put tooth paste on my toothrbush
achim-eneun chis-sol-e chiyag-eul ballat-eoyo

Emergency and Disasters – gingeubsanghwang- gwa jaehae

Emergency gingeubsanghwang
Help do-woom
Fire bul
Ambulance gugeubcha
First aid eung-geub cheochi
CPR - CPR simpyesosangsul
CPR - CPR simpyesosaengsul
Emergency number gingeub jeonhwabeonho
Accident sago / **Car crash** jadongcha chungdol
Death jug-eum / **Deadly** chimyeongjeog-in / **Fatality** samangja
Lightly wounded gyeongsang / **Moderately wounded** jungsang
Seriously wounded jungsang
Siren sailen
Fire truck sobangcha / **Fire extinguisher** sohwagi
Police gyeongchal / **Police station** gyeongchalseo
Robbery gangdo
Thief dodug

There is a fire. I need to call for help.
hwajaega balsaenghaetseubnida. doum-eul yocheonghaeya haeyo.
I need to call an ambulance.
gugeubchaleul bulleoya haeyo.
That accident was bad.
geu sagoneun nappatseubnida.
The car crash was fatal, there were two deaths, and four suffered serious injuries.
gyotongsagoga balsaenghae 2myeong-i samanghago 4myeong-i jungsang-eul ib-eotda.
One was moderately wounded and two were lightly wounded.
1myeong-eun jungsang, 2myeong-eun gyeongsang-eul ib-eotda.
CPR is a first step of first-aid.
simpyesosaengsul(CPR)eun eung-geubcheochiui cheos beonjjae dangyeibnida.
Please provide me with the emergency number.
gingeubjeonhwabeonholeul allyeojuseyo.
The police are on their way.
gyeongchal-i ogo it-eoyo.
I must call the police station to report a robbery.
gangdo sageon-eul singohalyeomyeon gyeongchalseoe jeonhwahaeya haeyo.
The siren of the fire truck is very loud.
sobangchaui sailen soliga neomu keuda.
Where is the fire extinguisher?
sohwagineun eodie itnayo?

Fire hydrant sohwajeon
Fireman sobangsu
Emergency situation gingeub sanghwang
Explosion pogbal
Rescue gujo
Natural disaster jayeon jaehae
Damage pihae / **Destruction** pagoe
Hurricane heolikein / **Tornado** taepung
Flood hongsu
Storm pogpung
Snowstorm nunbola
Hail woobag
Refuge pinan
Caused won-in
Safety anjeon
Drought gamum / **Famine** gigeun
Poverty bingon
Epidemic gam-yeombyeong yuhaeng
Pandemic gam-yeombyeong segyejeog yuhaeng

It's prohibited to park by the fire hydrant in case of a fire.
hwajae balsaeng si sohwajeon yeop-e juchahaneun geos-eun geumjidoeeo itseubnida.
When there is a fire, the first to arrive on scene are the firemen.
hwajaega balsaenghamyeon gajang meonjeo hyeonjang-e dochaghaneun salam-eun sobang-gwan-ida.
There is a fire. I must call for help.
hwajaega balsaenghaetseubnida. doum-eul yocheonghaeya haeyo.
In an emergency situation everyone needs to be rescued.
gingeub sanghwang-eseoneun moduleul gujohaeya habnida.
The gas explosion led to a natural disaster.
gaseu pogballo inhae jayeonjaehaega balsaenghaetseubnida.
The hurricane caused a lot of damage and destruction in its path.
heolikein-eun geu gyeonglo-e manh-eun pihaewa pagoeleul il-eukyeotseubnida.
The tornado destroyed the town.
toneidoga ma-eul-eul pagoehaetseubnida.
The drought led to famine and a lot of poverty.
gamum-eun gigeungwa manh-eun bingon-eul gajyeowatseubnida.
There were three days of flooding following the storm.
pogpung ihu 3il dong-an hongsuga balsaenghaetseubnida.
This is a snowstorm and not a hail storm.
igeos-eun ubag pogpung-i anila nunbolaibnida.

Dangerous wiheomhan
Danger wiheom
Warning gyeong-go
Earthquake jijin
Disaster jaehae
Disaster area jaehae jiyeog
Evacuation daepi
Mandatory pilsujeog-in
Safe place anjeonhan got
Blackout jeongjeon
Rainstorm bibalam
Lightning beongae
Thunder chun-dung
Avalanche nunsatae
Heatwave pog-yeom
Rip current ianlyu
Tsunami sseunami
Whirlpool soyongdol-i
Lightning beongae

We need to evacuate the buildings during the earthquake.
jijin-i balsaenghamyeon geonmul-eseo daepihaeya habnida.
Heatwaves are usually in the summer.
pog-yeom-eun daegae yeoleum-e balsaenghabnida.
This is a disaster area, therefore there is a mandatory evacuation order.
igos-eun jaehae jiyeog-imeulo gangje daepi myeonglyeong-i naelyeojyeo itseubnida.
Due to the rainstorm there was a blackout for three hours.
pog-ulo inhae 3sigan dong-an jeongjeon-i balsaenghaetseubnida.
Be careful during the snowstorm, because there might be an avalanche.
nunbolaga chineun nal-eneun nunsataega il-eonal su it-euni josimhaseyo.
There is a tsunami warning today.
oneul-eun sseunami gyeongboga ballyeongdoeeotseubnida.
You can't swim against a rip current.
ianlyue majseo suyeonghal suneun eobs-seubnida.
There is a dangerous whirlpool in the ocean.
bada-eneun wiheomhan soyongdol-iga itseubnida.
There is a risk of lightning today.
oneul-eun beongae wiheom-i itseubnida.

Home – jib

Living room geosil
Couch sopa
Sofa sopa
Door mun
Closet otjang
Stairway gyedan
Rug maet
Curtain keoteun
Window changmun
Floor badag
Floor (as in level) badag
Fireplace byuknanlo
Chimney gulttug
Oven obeun
Stove nanlo
Pot (cooking) naembi
Pan paen

The living room is missing a couch.
geosil-eneun sopaga eobs-seubnida.
I must buy a new door for my closet.
otjang-yong mun-eul saelo saya haeyo.
The spiral staircase is beautiful.
naseonhyeong gyedan-i aleumdabseubnida.
There aren't any curtains on the windows.
changmun-eneun keoteun-i eobs-seubnida.
I have a marble floor on the first floor and a wooden floor on the second floor.
1cheung-eun daeliseog badag, 2cheung-eun namu badag-eulo doeeo it-eoyo.
The fire sparkles in the fireplace.
byeognanlo-eseo bul-i banjjag-inda.
I can clean the floors today and then I want to arrange the closet.
oneul-eun badag-eul cheongsohan da-eum otjang-eul jeonglihago sip-eoyo.
I have to wash the rug with laundry detergent.
leogeuleul setagsejelo setaghaeya haeyo.
The pizza is in the oven.
pijaga obeun an-e it-eoyo.
The pots and pans are in the cabinet.
naembiwa peulaipaen-eun kaebinit an-e iteubnida.
The stove isn't functioning.
nanloga jagdonghaji anhseubnida.

Silverware eunjepum
Knife kal
Fork pokeu
Spoon sudgalag
Teaspoon tiseupun
Kitchen jubang
A cup keob
Plate jeopsi
Bowl geuleus
Napkin naebkin
Table tak-ja
Placemat sik-tak maeteu
Table cloth teibeulbo
Glass (material) yuli
A glass (cup) keob
Shelve seonban
Cabinet sunab-jang
Pantry siglyopum jeojangsil
Drawer seolab

The knives, spoons, teaspoons, and forks are inside the drawer in the kitchen.
kal, sudgalag, tiseupun, pokeuneun jubang seolab an-e it-eoyo.
There aren't enough cups, plates, and silverware on the table for everyone.
teibeul wie modeun salam-eul wihan keob, jeobsi, eunsiggilyuga chungbunhaji anhseubnida.
The napkin is underneath the bowl.
naebkin-eun geuleus mit-e it-eoyo.
The placemats are on the table.
Sik-takmaeteuneun teibeul wie it-eoyo.
The table cloth is beautiful.
teibeulboga yeppeuneyo.
There is canned food in the pantry.
siglyopum jeojangsil-e tongjolim sigpum-i itseubnida.
Where are the toothpicks?
issusigaeneun eodie itnayo?
The glasses on the shelve are used for champagne, not wine.
seonban-e itneun jan-eun wain-i anin syampein-eul damneun jan-ibnida.

Bedroom chimsil
Bed chimdae
Mattress maeteuris
Pillow - begae
Blanket dam-yo
Bed sheet chimdae siteu
Mirror geoul
Chair uija
Dinning room sigdang
Hallway hyeongwan
Downstairs alaecheung
Towel sugeon
Bathtub – yog-jo
Shower syawo
Sink singkeudae
Soap binu
Bathroom hwajangsil
Laundry ppallae
Candle yangcho

The master bedroom is at the end of the hallway, and the dining room is downstairs. keun chimsil-eun bogdo kkeut-e itgo, sigdang-eun alaecheung-e itseubnida.
The mirror looks good in the bedroom.
geoul-eun chimsil-e jal eoullibnida.
I have to buy a new bed and a new mattress.
sae chimdaewa sae maeteuliseuleul saya haeyo.
Where are the blankets and bed sheets?
dam-yowa chimdae siteuneun eodie itnayo?
My pillows are on the chair.
nae begaeneun uija wie it-eoyo.
These towels are for drying your hand.
i sugeon-eun son-eul malligi wihan geos-ibnida.
The bathtub, shower, and the sink are old.
yogjo, syawogi, semyeondaega nalg-atseubnida.
I need soap to wash my hands.
son-eul ssis-eulyeomyeon binuga pil-yohaeyo.
The guest bathroom is in the corner of the hallway.
sonnim-yong yogsil-eun bogdo motung-ie itseubnida.
I can only light this candle now.
jigumeun i chosbul-eman bul-eul but-il su it-eoyo.

Room bang
Balcony balkoni
Roof jibung
Ceiling cheonjang
Wall byeog
Carpet yangtanja
Attic dalag
Basement jiha
Trash sseulegi
Garbage can sseulegitong
Driveway chado
Garden jeong-won
Backyard dwitteul
Jar hang-ali
Doormat hyeongwan maeteu
Bag gabang
Box sangja
Keys yeolsoe

I can install new windows for my balcony.
balkonie sae changmun-eul seolchihal su itseubnida.
I must install a new roof.
sae jibung-eul seolchihaeya haeyo.
The color of my ceiling is white.
nae cheonjang-ui saegkkal-eun huinsaeg-ida.
I must paint the walls.
byeog-eul chilhaeya haeyo.
The attic is an extra room in the house.
dalagbang-eun jib-e itneun yeobun-ui gong-gan-ibnida.
The kids are playing either in the basement or the backyard.
aideul-eun jihasil-ina dwismadang-eseo nolgo itseubnida.
All the glass jars are outside on the doormat.
modeun yulibyeong-eun bakke-e hyeongwan maeteu-e itseubnida.
The garbage can is blocking the driveway.
sseulegitong-i jin-ibloleul maggo itseubnida.
How many boxes does he have?
geu salam-eun sangjaga myeoch gae itnayo?
I want to put my things in the plastic bag.
nae mulgeon-eul binilbongjie neohgo sip-eoyo.
I need to bring my keys.
yeolsoeleul gajyeowaya haeyo.

Conclusion

You have now learned a wide range of sentences in relation to a variety of topics such as the home and garden. You can discuss the roof and ceiling of a house, plus natural disasters like hurricanes and thunderstorms.

The combination of sentences can also work well when caught in a natural disaster and having to deal with emergency issues. When the electricity gets cut you can tell your family or friends, "I can only light this candle now." As you're running out of the house, remind yourself of the essentials by saying, "I need to bring my keys with me."

If you need to go to a hospital, you have now been provided with sentences and the vocabulary for talking to doctors and nurses and dealing with surgery and health issues. Most importantly, you can ask, "What is the emergency number in this country?" When you get to the hospital, tell the health services, "The hurricane caused a lot of destruction and damage in its path," and "We used the hurricane shelter for refuge."

The three hundred and fifty words that you learned in part 1 should have been a big help to you with these new themes. When learning the Korean language, you are now more able to engage with people in Korean, which should make your travels flow a lot easier.

Part 3 will introduce you to additional topics that will be invaluable to your journeys. You will learn vocabulary in relation to politics, the military, and the family. The three books in this series all together provide a flawless system of learning the Korean language. When you visit Korea, you will now have the capacity for greater conversational learning.

When you proceed to Part 3 you will be able to expand your vocabulary and conversational skills even further. Your range of topics will expand to the office environment, business negotiations and even school.

Please, feel free to post a review in order to share your experience or suggest feedback as to how this method can be improved.

Conversational Korean Quick and Easy
The Most Innovative Technique to Learn the Korean Language

Part III

YATIR NITZANY
And
VEDAT ATACAN

Introduction to the Program

You have now reached Part 3 of Conversational Korean Quick and Easy. In Part 1 you learned the 350 words that could be used in an infinite number of combinations. In Part 2 you moved on to putting these words into sentences. You learned how to ask for help when your house was hit by a hurricane and how to find the emergency services. For example, if you need to go to a hospital, you have now been provided with sentences and the vocabulary for talking to doctors and nurses and dealing with surgery and health issues. When you get to the hospital, you can tell the health services, "The hurricane caused a lot of destruction and damage in its path," and "We used the hurricane shelter for refuge."

In this third book in the series, you will find the culmination of this foreign language course that is based on a system using key phrases used in day-to-day life. You can now move on to further topics such as things you would say in an office. This theme is ideal if you've just moved to Korean for a new job. You may be about to sit at your desk to do an important task assigned to you by your boss but you have forgotten the details you were given. Turn to your colleagues and say, "I have to write an important email but I forgot my password." Then, if the reply is "Our secretary isn't here today. Only the receptionist is here but she is in the bathroom," you'll know what is being said and you can wait for help. By the end of the first few weeks, you'll have at your disposal terminology that can help reflect your experiences. "I want to retire already," you may find yourself saying at coffee break on a Monday morning after having had to go to your bank manager and say, "I need a small loan in order to pay my mortgage this month."

I came up with the idea of this unique system of learning foreign languages as I was struggling with my own attempt to learn Korean. When playing around with word combinations I discovered 350 words that when used together could make up an infinite number of sentences. From this beginning, I was able to start speaking in a new language. I then practiced and found that I could use the same technique with other languages, such as Spanish, French, Italian and Arabic. It was a revelation.

This method is by far the easiest and quickest way to master other languages and begin practicing conversational language skills.

The range of topics and the core vocabulary are the main components of this flawless learning method. In Part 3 you have a chance to learn how to relate to people in many more ways. Sports, for example, are very important for keeping healthy and in good spirits. The social component of these types of activities should not be underestimated at all. You will, therefore, have much help when you meet some new people, perhaps in a bar, and want to say to them, "I like to watch basketball games," and "Today are the finals of the Olympic Games. Let's see who wins the World Cup."

For sports, the office, and for school, some parts of conversation are essential. What happens when you need to get to work but don't have any clean clothes to wear because of malfunctions with the machinery. What you need is to be able to pick up the phone and ask a professional or a friend, "My washing machine and dryer are broken so maybe I can wash my laundry at the public laundromat." When you finally head out after work for some drinks and meet a nice new man, you can say, "You can leave me a voicemail or send me a text message."

Hopefully, these examples help show you how reading all three parts of this series in combination will prepare you for all you need in order to boost your conversational learning skills and engage with others in your newly learned language. The first two books have been an important start. This third book adds additional vocabulary and will provide the comprehensive knowledge required.

Office – samusil

Boss sajang
Employee jig-won / **Staff** jig-won
Meeting hoeui / **Conference room** hoeuisil
Secretary biseo / **Receptionist** jeobsuwon
Schedule iljeong / **Calendar** dallyeog
Supplies yongpum
Pen pen / **Ink** ingkeu
Pencil yeonpil / **Eraser** jiugae
Desk chaegsang
Cubicle kan-mag-i
Chair uija
Office furniture samuyong gagu
Business card myeongham
Lunch break jeomsim sigan
Days off hyuil
Briefcase seolyugabang
Bathroom hwajangsil

My boss asked me to hand in the paperwork.
sangsaga jae-ge seolyuleul jechulhalago haess-eoyo.
Our secretary isn't here today. The receptionist is here but she is in the bathroom.
oneul uli biseoga an wass-eoyo. jeobsuwon-eun yeogi itjiman geunyeoneun hwajangsil-e it-eoyo.
The employee meeting can take place in the conference room.
jig-won hoeuineun hoeuisil-eseo yeollil su itseubnida.
My business cards are inside my briefcase.
nae myeongham-eun seolyugabang an-e it-eoyo.
The office staff must check their work schedule daily.
samusil jig-won-eun maeil jasin-ui eobmu iljeong-eul hwag-inhaeya habnida.
I am going to buy office furniture.
naneun samuyong gaguleul salyeogo haeyo.
There isn't any ink in this pen.
i pen-eneun ingkeuga eobs-seubnida.
This pencil is missing an eraser.
i yeonpil-eneun jiugaega eobs-seubnida.
Our days off are written on the calendar.
uliui hyuil-eun dallyeog-e jeoghyeo itseubnida.
I need to buy extra office supplies.
samuyongpum-eul chugalo saya haeyo.
I am busy until lunch.
jeomsimttaekkaji bappayo

Laptop noteu-book
Computer keompyuteo
Keyboard keebodeu
Mouse mawooseu
Email imeil
Password bimilbeonho
Attachment chum-bu
Printer peulinteo/ **Colored printer** keolleopeulinteo
To download daunbad-da/ **To upload** eoblodeuhalyeomyeon
Internet inteonet
Account gyejeong
A copy sabon / **To copy** boksa-hada
Paste but-i-gi
Cut and paste boksa-wabut-yeoneohgi
Scanner seukaeneo / **To scan** seukaenhada / **Fax** paegseu
Telephone jeonhwa
A charger chungjeongi / **To charge** chungjeonhada

I have to write an important email but I forgot my password for my account.
jung-yohan imeil-eul jagseonghaeya haneunde gyejeong bimilbeonholeul ij-eobeolyeotseubnida.
I need to purchase a computer, a keyboard, a printer, and a desk.
keompyuteo, kibodeu, peulinteo, chaegsang-eul gu-ibhaeya habnida.
Where is the mouse for my laptop?
nae noteubug-yong mauseuneun eodie itnayo?
The internet is slow today therefore it's difficult to upload or download.
oneul-eun inteones sogdoga neulyeoseo eoblodeuna daunlodeuga eolyeobseubnida.
Do you have a colored printer?
keolleo peulinteoga itnayo?
I needed to fax the contract but instead, I decided to send it as an attachment in the email.
gyeyagseoleul paegseulo bonaeya haneunde daesin imeil-e cheombuhayeo bonaegilo haetseubnida.
One of these days, the fax machine will be completely obsolete.
eonjenganeun paegseu gigiga wanjeonhi sseulmo-eobsge doel geos-ibnida.
Where is my phone charger?
nae hyudaepon chungjeongineun eodie itnayo?
The scanner is broken.
seukaeneoga gojangnatseubnida.
The telephone is behind the chair.
jeonhwagineun uija dwie it-eoyo.

Shredder paswae-gi
Copy machine bogsagi
Filing cabinet seolyu kaebines
Paper jong-i
Page peiji
Paperwork seolyujag-eob
Portfolio poteupollio
Files pail
Document munseo
Contract gyeyag
Records gilog / **Archives** akaibeu
Deadline magam sigan
Binder baindeo
Paper clip jong-i keullib
Stapler hochikiseu / **Staples** hochikiseu
Stamp upyo / **Mail** upyeon
Letter pyeonji / **Envelope** bongtu
Data deiteo / **Analysis** bunseog
Highlighter hyeong-gwangpen
Marker pyosi/ **To highlight** gangjohada
Ruler ja

The supervisor at our company is responsible for data analysis.
uli hoesaui gamdogjaneun deiteo bunseog-eul damdanghabnida.
The copy machine is next to the telephone.
bogsagineun jeonhwagi yeop-e itseubnida.
The ruler is next to the shredder.
ja-neun paswaegi yeop-e itseubnida.
I can't find my stapler, paper clips, nor my highlighter in my cubicle.
nae kanmag-ieneun hochikisue jong-i keullib, hyeong-gwangpen-eul chaj-eul su eobs-seubnida.
The filing cabinet is full of documents.
seolyu kaebinis-eneun munseoga gadeughabnida.
The garbage can is full of papers.
sseulegitong-eneun jong-iga gadeughabnida.
Give me the file because today is the deadline.
oneul-i magam-inikka pail-eul juseyo.
Where do I put the binder?
baindeoneun eodie dunayo?
I need a stamp and an envelope.
upyowa bongtuga pil-yohaeyo.
There is a letter in the mail.
upyeonham-e pyeonjiga itseubnida.

School – haggyo

Student hagsaeng
Teacher seonsaengnim
Substitute teacher daeligyosa
A class su-up
A classroom gyosil
Education gyoyug
Private school salib haggyo
Public school gonglib haggyo
Elementary school chodeung haggyo
Middle school jung haggyo
High school godeung haggyo
University dae haggyo / **College** daehag
Grade hak-nyun / **Grade (grade on a test)** seongjeog
Pass tong-gwa / **Fail** - silpae
Absent gyeolseog / **Present** chulseog

The classroom is empty.
gyosil-i bieo itseubnida.
I want to bring my laptop to class today.
oneul sueob-e noteubug-eul gajyeogago sip-eoyo.
Our math teacher is absent and therefore a substitute teacher replaced him.
uli suhag seonsaengnim-i bujaehasyeoseo daeche seonsaengnim-i daesinhae jusyeoss-eoyo.
All the students are present.
modeun hagsaengdeul-i chulseoghaetseubnida.
Make sure to pass your classes because you can't fail this semester.
ibeon haggieneun nagjehal su eobs-euni kkog habgyeoghaseyo.
The education level at a private school is much more intense.
salibhaggyoui gyoyug sujun-eun hwolssin deo eomgyeoghabnida.
I went to a public elementary and middle school.
jeoneun gonglib chodeung haggyowa junghaggyoleul danyeoyseubnida.
I have good memories of high school.
naneun godeunghaggyo sijeol joh-eun gieog-eul gajgo itda.
You must get good grades on your report card.
seongjeogpyoe joh-eun seongjeog-eul bad-aya habnida.
My son is 15 years old and he is in the ninth grade.
je adeul-eun 15sal-igo 9hagnyeon-ieyo.
College textbooks are expensive.
daehag gyo-jaeneun bissada.
I want to study at an out-of-state university.
taju daehag gyo-eseo gongbuhago sipseubnida.

Subject gwamog
Science gwahag
Chemistry hwahag / **Physics** mullihag
Geography jilihag
History yeogsa
Math suhag
Addition deos-sem / **Subtraction** ppaegi
Division nanut-se / **Multiplication** gobsem
Language eon-eo / **English** yeong-eo / **Foreign language** oegug-eo
Physical education cheyug
Chalk bunpil / **Board** chilpan
Report card seongjeogpyo
Alphabet alpabet / **Letters** dan-eo/ **Words** dan-eo
To review geomto-hada
Dictionary sajeon
Detention gulgum / **The principle** won-chig

At school, geography is my favorite subject, English is easy, math is hard, and history is boring.
haggyoeseo jilineun naega gajang joh-ahaneun gwamog-igo, yeong-eoneun swibgo, suhag-eun eolyeobgo, yeogsaneun jiluhada.
After English class, there is physical education.
yeong-eo sueob hueneun cheyug sueob-i itseubnida.
Today's math lesson is on addition and subtraction.
oneul suhag sueob-eun deos-semgwa ppaelsem-ieyo.
Next month it will be division and multiplication.
da-eum dal-eneun nanus-semgwa gobsem-i naobnida.
This year for foreign language credits, I want to choose Spanish and Korean.
olhaeneun oegug-eo hagjeom-eulo seupein-eowa hangug-eoleul seontaeghago sipseubnida.
I want to buy a dictionary, thesaurus, and a journal for school.
haggyoeseo sseul sajeon, dong-uieo sajeon, ilgijang-eul sago sip-eoyo.
The teacher needs to write the homework on the board with chalk.
gyosaneun chilpan-e bunpillo sugjeleul sseoya habnida.
Today the students have to review the letters of the alphabet oneul
hagsaengdeul-eun alpabet geuljaleul bogseubhaeya habnida.
The teacher wants to teach roman numerals.
seonsaengnim-i lomasutjaleul galeuchigo sip-eohaeyo.
If you can't behave then you must go to the principal's office, and maybe stay after school for detention.
haengdonghal su eobsdamyeon gyojangsillo gaya hago bang-gwa huenam-a it-eul sudo itseubnida.

Test siheom / **Quiz** kwijeu
Lesson sueob / **Notes** memo
Homework sugje / **Assignment** gwaje / **Project** peulojegteu
Backpack baenang
Book chaeg
Folders poldeo / **Notebook** gongchaeg / **Papers** jong-i
Calculator gyesangi
Glue pul / **Adhesive tape** jeobchag teipeu / **Scissors** gawi
Lunchbox jeomsim dosilag / **Lunch** jeomsim / **Cafeteria** gunae sigdang
Kindergarten yuchiwon / **Pre-school** yuchiwon / **Day care** tag-a-so
Triangle samgaghyeong / **Square** jeongsagaghyeong / **Circle** won
Crayons keuleyong

Today, we don't have a test but we have a surprise quiz.
oneul-eun siheom-eun eobsjiman kkamjjag kwijeuleul junbihaetseubnida.
Are a pen, a pencil, and an eraser included with the school supplies?
hag-yongpum-eneun pen, yeonpil, jiugaega pohamdoeeo itnayo?
I think my notepad and calculator are in my backpack.
nae baenang an-e memojang-gwa gyesangiga deul-eo itneun geos gat-ayo.
All my papers are in my folder.
nae modeun seolyu-ga poldeo-an-ae itseubnida.
I need glue and scissors for my project.
nae peulojegteue pulgwa gawiga pil-yohaeyo.
I need tape and a stapler to fix my book.
chaeg-eul gochilyeomyeon teipeuwa hochikiseuga pil-yohaeyo.
You have to concentrate in order to take notes.
memoleul halyeomyeon jibjunghaeya habnida.
The school librarian wants to invite the art and music teacher to the library next week.
haggyo saseoneun da-eum jue misul miteum-ag gyosaleul doseogwan-e chodaehago sip-eohabnida.
For lunch, your children can purchase food at the cafeteria or they can bring food from home.
jeomsim sigan-eneun janyeoga gunaesigdang-eseo eumsig-eul gu-ibhageona jib-eseo eumsig-eul gajyeool su itseubnida.
I forgot my lunchbox and crayons at home.
jib-e dosilaggwa keuleyong-eul ij-eobeolyeoss-eoyo.
To draw shapes such as a triangle, square, circle, and rectangle is easy.
samgaghyeong, jeongsagaghyeong, wonhyeong, jigsagaghyeong deung-ui dohyeong-eul geulineun geos-eun swibseubnida.
During the week, my youngest child is at daycare, my middle one is in pre-school, and the oldest is in kindergarten.
jujung-e magnae aineun eolin-ijib-e, dul-jaeaineun yuchiwon-e, keun aineun yuchiwon-e gabnida.

Profession - jig-eob

Doctor uisa / **Nurse** ganhosa / **Veterinarian** suuisa
Psychologist simlihagja / **Psychiatrist** jeongsingwa uisa
Lawyer byeonhosa / **Judge** pansa
Pilot jojongsa / **Flight attendant** seungmuwon
Reporter lipoter / **Journalist** gija
Electrician jeongigong / **Mechanic** jeongbigong
Investigator josaja / **Detective** hyeongsa / **Translator** beonyeog-ga
Producer jejagja/ **Director** gamdog

What's your profession?
dangsin-ui jig-eob-eun mueot-ibnikka?
I am going to medical school to study medicine because I want to be a doctor.
naneun uisaga doego sip-eoseo uihag-eul gongbuhagi wihae uigwadaehag-e gal geoyeyo.
There is a difference between a psychologist and a psychiatrist.
simlihagjawa jeongsingwa uisa-eneun chaiga itseubnida.
Most children want to be an astronaut, a veterinarian, or an athlete.
daebubun-ui aideul-eun ujubihaengsa, suuisa, undongseonsuga doegileul wonhabnida.
The judge spoke to the lawyer at the court house.
pansaneun beob-won-eseo byeonhosawa iyagileul nanwotseubnida.
The police investigator needs to investigate this case.
gyeongchal susagwan-eun i sageon-eul josahaeya handa.
Being a detective could be a fun job.
hyeongsaga doeneun geos-eun jaemiissneun jig-eob-i doel su itseubnida.
The flight attendant and the pilot are on the plane.
seungmuwongwa jojongsaga bihaeng-gi-e itseubnida.
I am a certified electrician.
jeoneun jeongigisa jagyeog-eul gajchun salam-ibnida.
The mechanic overcharged me.
jeongbigong-i na-ege gwadohan biyong-eul cheong-guhaetseubnida.
I want to be a journalist.
naneun jeoneolliseuteuga doego sipda.
The best translators work at my company.
uli hoesa-eneun choegoui beon-yeoggadeul-i ilhago itseubnida.
Are you a photographer?
dangsin-eun sajin jaggaibnikka?
The author wants to write a book.
Jag-ganeun chaeg-eul sseugo sip-eohabnida.
I want to find the directors of the company.
hoesaui isaleul chajgo sipseubnida.

Artist (performer) yesulga/ **Artist (draws paints picture)** hwaga
Author jagga / **Writer** jagga
Painter hwaga
Dancer daenseo
Photographer sajinjagga
A cook yolisa / **Waiter** weiteo / **Bartender** batendeo
Barber ibalsa / **Barber shop** ibalso / **Stylist** stail-listeu
Housekeeper gajeongbu / **Maid** hanyeo
Caretaker ganbyeong-in
Farmer nongbu
Agriculturer nongbu
Gardner jeong-wonsa
Mailman upyeon jibbaewon
A guard gyeongbiwon
A cashier gyesan-won

The artist drew a sketch.
hwaganeun seukechileul geulyeotseubnida.
The artist produced new artwork for her catalog.
yesulganeun jasin-ui katallogeuleul wihae saeloun jagpum-eul jejaghaetseubnida.
I want to apply as a cook at the restaurant instead of as a waiter.
weiteo daesin leseutolang yolisalo jiwonhago sipseubnida.
The gardener can only come on weekdays.
jeong-wonsaneun pyeong-il-eman ol su itseubnida.
I have to go to the barbershop now.
naneun jigeum ibalso-e gaya haeyo.
Being a bartender isn't an easy job.
batendeoga doeneun geos-eun swiun il-i anibnida.
Why do we need another maid?
wae daleun hanyeoga pil-yohangayo?
I need to file a complaint against the mailman.
uchebuege bulman-eul jegihaeya habnida.
I am a part-time painter.
naneun siganje hwagaibnida.
She was a dancer at the theater play.
geunyeoneun yeongeug-ui daenseoyeotseubnida.
You need to contact the insurance company if you want to find another caretaker.
daleun ganbyeong-in-eul chaj-eulyeomyeon boheomhoesa-e mun-uihaeya habnida.
The farmer can sell us ripened tomatoes today.
nongbuneun oneul uliege jal ig-eun tomatoleul pal su itseubnida.

Business - sa-eob

A business il/ **company** hoesa / **Factory** gongjang
A professional jeonmunga
Position wichi / **Work** il / **job** jig-eob
Employee jig-won
Manager gwanlija / **Management** gwanli / **Owner** soyuja
Secretary biseo
An interview inteobyu / **Résumé** i-ryeog-seo
Presentation peulejenteisyeon
Specialist jeonmunga
To hire goyonghada / **To fire** jaluda
Pay check wol-geup/ **Income** su-ib / **Salary** wol-geup
Insurance boheom / **Benefits** iig
Trimester sam bungi / **Budget** yesan
Net sun/ **Gross** sun
To retire euntoehada / **Pension** yeongeum

I need a job.
naneun jig-eob-i pil-yohae.
She is the secretary of the company.
geunyeoneun hoesaui biseoibnida.
The manager needs to hire another employee.
gwanlijaneun daleun jig-won-eul goyonghaeya habnida.
I am lucky because I have an interview for a cashier position today.
oneul gyesan-won myeonjeob-i it-eoseo un-i johneyo.
How much is the salary and does it include benefits?
geub-yeoneun eolmaigo sudangdo pohamdoenayo?
Management has your resumé and they need to show it to the owner of the company.
gyeong-yeongjin-eun gwihaui ilyeogseoleul gajigo iss-eumyeo ileul hoesa soyujuege boyeojueoya habnida.
I am at work at the factory now.
jeoneun jigeum gongjang-eseo ilhago it-eoyo.
In business, you should be professional.
sa-eob-eseoneun jeonmungaga doeeoya habnida.
Is the presentation ready?
peulejenteisyeon junbidwaessnayo?
The first trimester is part of the annual budget.
cheorsambungineun yeongan yesan-ui ilbu-ibnida.
I have to see the net and gross profits of the business.
sa-eob-ui sun-iiggwa chong iig-eul hwag-inhaeya habnida.
I want to retire already.
naneun beolsseo euntoehago sipda

Client gogaeg
Broker beulokeo / **Salesperson** yeong-eobsawon
Realtor jung-gaein / **Real Estate** budongsan
A purchase gumae/ **A lease** imdae / **To lease** imdaehada
To invest tujahada/**Economy** gyeongje
Mortgage dae-chul/ **Interest rate** ijayul / **A loan** daechul
Commission susulyo / **Percent** peosenteu
Value gachi/**A sale** seil / **Profit** iig
Landlord ju-in / **Tenant** geojuja
The demand suyo / **The supply** gong-geub
A contract gyeyag
Terms jogun/**Signature** seomyeong/**Initials** seoyeong
Advertisement gwang-go

I can earn a huge profit from the stock market.
naneun jusigsijang-eseo keun iig-eul eod-eul su itda.
The demand in the real estate market depends on the economy.
budongsan sijang-ui suyoneun gyeongjee ttala dallajibnida.
If you want to sell your home, I can recommend a very good realtor.
jib-eul palgo sipdamyeon aju joh-eun budongsan jung-gaein-eul chucheonhae deulil su itseubnida.
The investor wants to invest in this shopping center because he says it has good potential.
tujajaneun i syopingsenteoga joh-eun jamjaelyeog-eul gajgo issgi ttaemun-e i syopingsenteoe tujahago sip-eohabnida.
The value of the property increased by twenty percent.
budongsan gachiga 20peosenteu jeung-gahaetseubnida.
How much is the commission on the sale?
panmae susulyoneun eolmaingayo?
The client wants to lease instead of purchasing the property.
gogaeg-eun budongsan-eul gumaehaneun daesin imdaeleul wonhabnida.
What are the terms of the purchase?
 gumae jogeon-eun mueos-ibnikka?
I can negotiate a better interest rate.
deo na-eun ijayul-eul hyeobsanghal su itseubnida.
I need a small loan in order to pay my mortgage this month.
ibeon dal jutaegdambodaechulgeum-eul jibulhalyeomyeon soaeg daechul-i pil-yohabnida.
I need a signature and an initial on the contract.
gyeyagseoe seomyeong-ipil-yohabnida.
My position in the company is marketing and I am responsible for advertising and ads.
hoesa-eseo jeoui jig-wineun maketing-imyeo, gwang-go mich gwang-go eobmuleul damdanghago itseubnida.

Money don / **Currency** tonghwa
Cash hyeongeum / **Coins** dongjeon
Change (change for a bill) jandon
Credit sin-yong geolae
Tax se
Price gagyeog
Invoice songjang
Inventory moglog
Merchandise sangpum
A refund hwanbul
A product jepum
Produced saengsan
Retail somae
Wholesale domae
Imports su-ib / **Exports** suchul
To ship baesonghada / **Shipment** seonjeog

Don't forget to bring cash with you.
hyeongeum-eul jichamhaneun geos-eul ij-ji maseyo.
Do you have change for a $100 bill?
100dalleojjali jipye jandon-i itnayo?
I don't have a credit card.
sin-yongkadeuga eobs-eoyo.
The salesperson told me there is no refund.
panmaewon-i hwanbul-i andoendago hadeogun-yo.
This product is produced in Italy.
i jepum-eun itallia-eseo saengsandoebnida.
I work in the export/import business.
jeoneun suchul-ib-eob-e jongsahago itseubnida.
Let me check my inventory.
nae inbentolileul hwag-inhae bogetseubnida.
This product is covered by insurance.
bon sangpum-eun boheom-i jeog-yongdoeneun sangpum-ibnida.
This invoice contains a mistake.
i cheong-guseoe silsuga itseubnida.
What is the wholesale and retail value of this shipment?
i balsongmul-ui domae mit somae gagyeog-eun eolmaibnikka?
You don't have enough money to purchase the merchandise.
sangpum-eul gumaehal don-i bujoghabnida.
How much does the shipping cost and is it in US currency?
baesong biyong-eun eolmaimyeo migug tonghwalo pyosidoebnikka?
There is a tax exemption on this income.
i sodeug-eneun segeum myeonjega itseubnida.

Sports – Seupocheu

Basketball nonggu / **Soccer** chuggu / **Ball** gong / **Basket** basuket
Game geim / **Stadium** gyeong-gijang
Player seonsu
To jump jeompeuhada / **To throw** deonjida / **To kick** chada
To catch jabda
Coach kochi / **Referee** simpan / **Competition** gyeongjaeng
Team tim / **Teammate** tim-won / **National team** gugga daepyotim
Opponent sangdae
Half time hapeu taim / **Finals** gyeolseung
Score jeomsu / **Scores** jeomsu
Goal gol / **The goal** mogpyo
To lose ilhda / **A Defeat** paebae
To win igida / **A victory** seungli
The looser paebaeja / **The winner** seungja
Fans paen / **Field** pildeu / **Helmet** helmes / **Whistle** holulagi
Penalty paeneolti

I like to watch basketball games.
naneun nong-gu gyeong-gileul boneun geos-eul joh-ahabnida.
Soccer is my favorite sport.
chugguneun naega gajang joh-ahaneun seupocheu-ida.
I have tickets to a football game at the stadium.
naneun gyeong-gijang-eseo yeollineun chuggu gyeong-gi tikes-eul gajigo itseubnida.
To play basketball, you need to be good at shooting and jumping.
nong-guleul halyeomyeon syuting-gwa jeompeuleul jalhaeya habnida.
The national team has a lot of fans.
guggadaepyoeneun paen-i manhda.
My teammate can't find his baseball helmet.
nae tim donglyoga yagu helmes-eul chaj-ji moshaetseubnida.
The coach and the team were on the field during half-time.
kochiwa tim-eun hapeutaim dong-an pildeue it-eotseubnida.
The coach needs to bring his team today to meet the new referee.
kochineun oneul sae simpan-eul mannagi wihae geuui tim-eul delyeowaya habnida.
Our opponents went home after their defeat.
uliui sangdaetim-eun paebae hu jib-eulo dol-agatseubnida.
The player received a penalty for kicking the ball in the wrong goal.
geu seonsuneun jalmosdoen gol-e gong-eul chaseo peneoltileul bad-assseubnida.
Not every person likes sports.
modeun salam-i seupocheuleul joh-ahaneun geos-eun anibnida.

Athlete undong seonsu / **Olympics** ollimpig / **World cup** woldeukeob
Bicycle jajeongeo / **Cyclist** saicul-list
Swimming suyeong
Wrestling leseulling / **Boxing** gwontu / **Martial arts** musul
Championship seonsugwon daehoe / **Trainer** hunlyeonja
Award sang Tournament toneomeonteu
Horse racing gyeongma / **Racing** gyeongju
Exercise undong / **Fitness** pitunis / **Gym** cheyuggwan
Captain jujang / **Judge** simpan / **A match** gyeong-gi / **Rules** gyuchig
Pool (billiards) dang-gu / **Pool (swimming pool)** suyeongjang

Today are the finals for the Olympic Games.
oneul-eun ollimpig geim-ui gyeolseungjeon-ibnida.
Let's see who wins the World Cup.
nuga woldeukeob-eseo igyeossneunji bobsida.
I want to compete in the cycling championship.
saikeulling chaempieonsib-eseo gyeongjaenghago sipseubnida.
I am an athlete so I must stay in shape.
naneun undong seonsu-imeulo mommaeleul yujihaeyahabnida.
After my boxing lesson, I want to go and swim in the pool.
gwontu sueob hu, naneun suyeongjang-eseo gaseo suyeonghago sipda.
He will receive an award because he is the winner of the martial-arts tournament.
geuneun musul toneomeonteuui useungjaigi ttaemun-e sang-eul bad-assseubnida.
The wrestling captain must teach his team the rules of the sport.
leseulling juuang-eun geuui tim-ege seupocheuui gyuchig-eul galeuchyeoyahabnida.
At the horse-racing competition, the judge couldn't announce the score.
gyeongma gyeongjaeng-eseo simpaneun jeomsuleul balpyo hal su eobs-eossseubnida.
There is a bicycle race at the park today.
oneul gong-won-eseo jajeongeo gyeongjuga itseubnida.
This fitness program is expensive.
i piteuniseu peulogeulaem-eun bissada.
It's healthy to go to the gym every day.
maeil cheyuggwan-eganeun geos-i geonganghabnida.
Weightlifting is good exercise.
yeogdoneun joh-eun undong-ibnida.
I want to run on the track today.
oneul teulaeg-eseo dalligo sip-eoyo.
I like to win in billiards.
naneun dang-gueseoigineun geos-eul joh-ahabnida.

Outdoor Activities - yaoe hwaldong

Hiking deungsan / **Hiking trail** deungsanlo
Pocket knife jumeoni-kal / **Compass** nachimban
Camping kaemping / **A camp** kaempeu
RV - Camping Car / **RV**- kaemping cha
Campground kaempeujang / **Tent** tenteu
Campfire modakbul
Matches seongnyang / **Lighter** laiteo
Coal seogtan / **Flame** bulkkoch / **The smoke** yeongi
Fishing nakksie / **To fish** nakksiehada
Fishing pole nakksi-dae / **Fishing line** nakksi-jul
Hook hug / **A float** jji / **A weight** chu / **Bait** mikki
Fishing net nakksi geumul
To hunt sanyanghada / **Rifle** sochong

I enjoy hiking on the trail, with my compass and my pocketknife.
naneun nachimbangwa jumeoni kalnallo teuleil-eseo haiking-eul jeulgibnida.
Don't forget the water bottle in your backpack.
baenang-ui mulbyeong-eul ij-ji masibsio.
There aren't any tents at the campground.
kaempeujang-eneun tenteuga eobs-seubnida.
I want to sleep in an RV instead of a tent.
naneun tenteu daesin RVeseo jago sipda.
We can use a lighter to start a campfire.
ulineun laiteoleul sayonghayeo kaempeu paieoleul sijaghal su itseubnida. **We need coal and matches for the camping trip.**
ulineun kaemping yeohaeng-eul wihae seogtangwa gyeong-giga pil-yohabnida.
Put out the fire because the flames are very high and there is a lot of smoke.
bulkkoch-i maeu nopgo yeongiga manhgi ttaemun-e bul-eul naelibnida.
There is fog outside and the temperature is below freezing.
oebu angaega itgo ondoneun eol-eo butseubnida.
Where is the fishing store?
nakksi gageneun eodie itseubnikka?
I need to buy hooks, fishing line, bait, and a net.
goli, nakksi-jul, mikki mit geumul-eul sayahabnida.
You can't bring your fishing pole or your hunting rifle to the campground of the State Park because there is a sign there which says, "No fishing and no hunting."
"nakksi gumjisanyang gjumji"ilaneun pyosiga itgi ttaemun-e julib gong-won-ui kaempeujang-eulo nakksisdae na sanyang sochong-eul gajyeool su eobs-seubnida.

Sailing hanghae / **A sail** doch / **Sailboat** yoteu
Rowing loing / **A paddle** paedeul
Motor moteo
Canoe kanu
Rock climbing ambyeogdeungban
Horseback riding seungma
Diver jamsubu / **Scuba diving** seukubeo daibing
Skydiving seukai daibing / **Parachute** naghasan
Paragliding paeleogeullaiding
Hot air balloon yeolgigu
Kite yeon
Surfing seoping / **Surf board** seoping bodeu
Ice skating aiseu seukeiting / **Skiing** seuki tagi

With a broken motor, we need a paddle to row the boat.
moteoga gojangnaseo boteuleul jeosgi wihaeseoneun noga pil-yohabnida.
It's important to know how to use a sail before sailing on a sailboat.
beomseon-eul tago hanghaehagi jeon-e doch sayongbeob-eul aneun geos-i jung-yohabnida.
In my opinion, a kayak is much more fun than a canoe.
je saeng-gag-en kayag-i kanuboda hwolssin deo jaemiit-eoyo.
Do I need to bring my scuba certification in order to scuba dive at the reef?
sanhocho-eseo seukubeo daibing-eul halyeomyeon seukubeo jagyeogjeung-eul gajyeowaya habnikka?
I have my mask, snorkel, and fins.
maseukeu, seunokeul, pin-i ir-eoyo.
I don't know which is scarier, sky diving or paragliding.
seukaidaibing-gwa paeleogeullaiding jung eoneu geos-i deo museounji moleugetseubnida.
There are several outdoor activities here including rock climbing and horseback riding.
igos-eseoneun ambyeog deungban, seungma deung dayanghan yaoe hwaldong-eul jeulgisil su itseubnida.
My dream was always to fly in a hot-air balloon.
nae kkum-eun hangsang yeolgiguleul tago nal-aganeun geos-ieotseubnida.
We are going skiing on our next vacation.
ulineun da-eum hyuga-e seukileul taleo gal yejeong-ida.
Where is the surfboard? I want to surf the waves at the beach tomorrow.
seopingbodeuneun eodie itnayo? naeil haebyeon-eseo padotagileul hago sip-eoyo.
Ice skating is fun.
aiseu seukeiting-eun jaemiiss-eoyo.

Electrical Devices - jeongi jangchi

Electricity jeongi / **Electric** jeongi
Appliance gigu
Oven obeun / **Stove** nanlo / **Microwave** jeonja-leinji
Refrigerator naengjang-go
Freezer naengdong-go
Coffee maker keopi meikeo / **Coffee pot** keopi poteu
Toaster toseuteoe
Dishwasher siggi secheoggi
Laundry machine setaggi / **Laundry** ppallae / **Dryer** geonjogi
Fan paen / **Air condition** aeaeocon
Alarm alam
Smoke detector yeongi gamjigi / **Remote Control** limokon
Battery baeteoli

He needs to pay his electric bill if he wants electricity.
geuneun jeongileul wonhamyeon jeongi yogeum-eul jibulhaeya habnida.
I need to purchase a few things at the electronic store and at the appliance store tomorrow.
naeil jeonjajepum maejang-gwa gajeonjepum maejang-eseo myeoch gaji mulgeon-eul saya haeyo.
I can't put plastic utensils in the dishwasher.
siggisecheoggie peullaseutig siggileul neoh-eul su eobs-eoyo.
I am going to get rid of my microwave and oven because they are not functioning.
jeonjaleinjiwa obeun-i jagdonghaji anh-aseo eobs-aelyeogo habnida.
The refrigerator and freezer aren't cold enough.
naengjang-gowa naengdong-goga chungbunhi chagabji anhseubnida.
The coffee maker and toaster aren't in the kitchen.
keopi meikeowa toseuteoneun jubang-e eobs-seubnida.
My washing machine and dryer do not function therefore I must wash my laundry at the public laundromat.
setaggiwa geonjogiga jagdonghaji anh-a gong-yongsetagsil-eseo setaghaeya habnida.
Is this fan new?
i paen-eun sae geoya?
Unfortunately, the new air conditioner unit hasn't been delivered yet.
antakkabgedo sae eeokeon jangchiga ajig baesongdoeji anh-atseubnida.
Is that annoying sound the alarm clock or the fire alarm?
geu jjajeungnaneun solineun allamsigyeinga, animyeon hwajae gyeongbogiinga?
The smoke detector needs new batteries.
yeongi gamjigieneun sae baeteoliga pil-yohabnida.

Stereo seutele-o
A clock sigye / **A watch** sigye
Vacuum cleaner cheongsogi
Phone haendeupon
Text message munja meseji / **Voice message** eumseong mesiji
Camera kamela
Flashlight peullaesi / **Light** bich / **Lamp** laempeu
Furnace yong-gwang-lo / **Heater** hiteo
Cord kodeu / **Charger** chungjeongi / **Outlet** konsenteu
Headsets hedeuses
Door bell choinjong
Lawn mower jandi kkakkneun gigye

The clock is hanging on the wall.
sigyega byeog-e geollyeo it-eoyo.
The cordless stereo is on the table.
museon seutele-oga teibeul wie it-eoyo.
I still have a home telephone.
naneun ajigdo jib jeonhwaleul gajigo itda.
I need to buy a lamp and a vacuum cleaner today.
oneul-eun laempeuwa jingongcheongsogileul saya haeyo.
In the past, cameras were more common.
gwageoeneun kamelaga deo ilbanjeog-ieotseubnida.
Today, everyone can use their phones to take pictures.
oneulnal-eneun nuguna hyudaepon-eul sayonghayeo sajin-eul jjig-eul su itseubnida.
You can leave me a voice message or send me a text message.
eumseong mesijileul namgigeona munja mesijileul bonaesil su itseubnida.
The lights don't function when there is a blackout therefore I must rely on my flashlight.
jeongjeon-i doemyeon jomyeong-i jagdonghaji anh-eumeulo sonjeondeung-e uijonhaeya habnida.
I can't hear the doorbell.
choinjong soliga deulliji anhseubnida.
There is a higher risk of causing a house fire from an electric heater than a furnace.
nanloboda jeongihiteolo inhae jib-e hwajaega balsaenghal wiheom-i deo nopseubnida.
I need to connect the cord to the outlet.
kodeuleul konsenteue yeongyeolhaeya haeyo.
His lawnmower is very noisy.
geuui jandi kkakkneun gigyeneun maeu sikkeuleobseubnida.
Why is my headset on the floor?
hedeuses-i badag-e itneun iyuneun mueos-ingayo?

Tools – dogu

Toolbox gong-gu sangja
Carpenter mogsu
Hammer mangchi /**Saw** tob/**Axe** dokki
A drill deulil /**To drill** gumeong-eul ttul-da
Nail mot /**A screw** nasa
Screwdriver deulaibeo
A wrench lenchi /**Pliers** penchi
Paint brush peinteu but /**To paint** chilhada /**The paint** peinteu
Ladder sadali
Rope lopeu /**String** kkeun
A scale jeo-wool
Measuring tape julja
Machine gigye
A lock jamulsoe /**Locked** jamgim /**To lock** jamgeudaAs
Equipment jangbi
Broom bitjaroo
Dust pan sseule-badgi
Bucket yangdong-i/**Sponge** seupeonji /**Mop** daegeolle
Shovel sab /**A trowel** mojong-sab

The carpenter needs nails, a hammer, a saw, and a drill.
mogsuegeneun mot, mangchi, tob, deulil-i pil-yohabnida.
The string is very long. Where are the scissors?
kkeun-i eomcheong gil-eoyo. gawineun eodie itnayo?
The screwdriver is in the toolbox.
deulaibeoneun dogu sangja-e itseubnida.
This tool can cut through metal.
i doguneun geumsog-eul jeoldanhal su itseubnida.
The ladder is next to the tools.
sadalineun dogu yeop-e issseubnida.
I must buy a brush to paint the walls.
byeog-eul chilhalyeomyeon bus-eul saya haeyo.
The paint bucket is empty.
peinteu tong-i bieo itseubnida.
It's better to tie the shovel with a rope in my pick up truck.
nae pig-eob teuleog-e sab-eul basjullo mukkneun geos-i deo johseubnida.
How can I fix this machine?
i gigyeleul eotteohge gochil su issnayo?
The broom and dust pan are with the rest of my cleaning equipment.
bisjaluwa sseulebadgineun nameoji cheongso doguwa hamkke itseubnida.
Where did you put the mop and the bucket?
daegeollewa yangdong-ineun eodie dueossnayo?

Car – cha / jadongcha

Engine enjin
Ignition si-ding
Steering wheel haen-deul
Automatic jadong/ **Manual** sudong
Gear shift byeon-sog geo
Seat jwaseog
Seat belt anjeon belteu
Airbag eeobaeg
Brakes beuleikeu
Handbrake haendeu beuleikeu
Baby seat yuayong jwaseog
Driver seat unjeonseog
Passenger seat seung-gaegseog
Front seat ap jwaseog
Back seat dwijjog jwaseog
Car passenger jadongcha seung-gaeg
Warning light gyeong-godeung
Button beo-tun
Horn (of the car) gyeongjeog

When driving, both hands must be on the steering wheel.
unjeonhal ttaeneun yangson-i haen-deulwil-eul jabgo it-eoya habnida.
I must take my car to my mechanic because there is a problem with the ignition.
Si-dong-emunjega it-eoseo chaleul jeongbisa-ege gajyeogaya habnida.
What happened to the engine?
enjin-eun eotteohge dwaessnayo?
The seat is missing a seat belt.
jwaseog-e anjeonbelteuga eobs-seubnida.
I prefer a gear shift instead of an automatic car. jeoneun
jadongbyeonsoggibodaneun gieobyeonsog-eul seonhohabnida.
The brakes are new in this vehicle
i chalyang-ui beuleikeuneun sae jepum-ibnida.
This vehicle doesn't have a handbrake.
i chalyang-eneun haendeu beuleikeuga eobs-seubnida.
There is an airbag on both the driver side and the passenger side.
unjeonseoggwa josuseog yangjjog-e eeobaeg-i itseubnida.
The baby seat is in the back seat.
yuayong kasiteuneun dwisjwaseog-e itseubnida.
The warning light button is located next to the stirring wheel.
gyeong-godeung beoteun-eun gyoban hwil yeop-e itseubnida.

Windshield balammag-i yuli
Windshield wiper ap yuli waipeo
Windshield fluid ap-yuli saechugjae
Rear view mirror baegmileo
Side mirror saideu mileo
Door handle mun sonjab-i
Spare tire seupeeo taieo
Trunk teuleongkeu
Hood (of the vehicle) hudeu
Alarm gyeongbo
Window chang
Driver license unjeonmyeonheojeung
License plate beonhopan
Gas gaseu
Low fuel jeo yeonbi
Flat tire balam ppajin taieo
Crowbar soe jilet-dae
A (car) jack cha-ryang talchui
Wrench lenchi

The windshield and all four of my car windows are cracked.
ap yuliwa jadongcha changmun naegaega modu kkaejyeotseubnida.
I want to clean my rear-view mirror and my side mirrors.
baegmileowa saideumileoleul cheongsohago sip-eoyo.
My car doesn't have an alarm.
nae cha-eneun allam-i eobs-seubnida.
Does this car have a spare tire in the trunk?
i cha teuleongkeue seupeeo taieoga itnayo?
Please, close the car door.
chamun-eul dad-ajuseyo.
Where is the nearest gas station?
gajang gakkaun juyusoneun eodie itnayo?
The windshield wipers are new.
ap-yuli waipeoneun saegeos-ibnida.
The door handle on the driver's side is broken.
unjeonseogjjog do-eosonjab-iga pasondoeeotseubnida.
Your license plate has expired.
gwihaui beonhopan-i manlyodoeeotseubnida.
I want to renew my driving license today.
oneul unjeonmyeonheojeung-eul gaengsinhago sip-eoyo.
Are the car doors locked?
jadongcha mun-eun jamgyeo itnayo?

Nature – jayeon

A plant sigmul
Forest sup
Tree namu
Wood mogjae
Trunk julgi /**Branch** namusgaji /**Leaf** ip /**Root** ppuli
Flower kkoch /**Petal** kkoch-ip /**Blossom** kkoch
Stem julgi /**Seed** ssiat
Rose jangmi
Nectar ggul/**Pollen** hwabun
Vegetation chomog
Bush gwanmog /**Grass** jandi
Rain forest yeoldaeulim / **Tropical** yeolldae /**Palm tree** yajasu
Season gyejeol
Spring bom /**Summer** yeoleum /**Winter** gyeoul /**Autumn** ga-eul

I want to collect a few leaves during the fall.
ga-eul-e namus-ip myeoch gaeleul mo-eugo sipseubnida.
There aren't any plants in the desert during this season.
i gyejeol-eneun samag-e sigmul-i hanado eobs-seubnida.
The trees need rain.
namueneun biga pil-yohabnida.
The trunk, the branches, and the roots are all parts of the tree.
julgi, gaji, ppulineun modu namuui ilbu-ibnida.
My rose bushes are beautiful.
nae jangmi deombul-eun aleumdabseubnida.
Where can I plant the seeds?
ssiat-eul eodie sim-eul su itnayo?
I must trim the grass in my garden.
naneun jeong-won-e itneun jandileul dadeum-eoya habnida.
The rain forest is a nature preserve.
yeoldae ulim-eun jayeon boho guyeog-ibnida.
Palm trees can only grow in a tropical climate.
yajasuneun yeoldae gihueseoman jalal su itseubnida.
I am allergic to pollen.
naneun kkochgalu alleleugiga itseubnida.
The orchid needs to bloom because I want to see its beautiful petals.
nanchoui aleumdaun kkoch-ip-eul bogo sipgi ttaemun-e nanchoga pieoya habnida.
Is the nectar from the flower sweet?
kkoch-ui kkul-eun dalkomhabnikka?
Be careful because the plant stem can break very easily.
sigmul julgiga maeu swibge buleojil su it-eumeulo juuihaseyo.

Lake hosu
Sea bada / **Ocean** daeyang
Waterfall pogpo
River gang / **Canal** unha / **Swamp** neup
Mountain san / **Hill** eondeog / **Cliff** nangtteoleoji / **Peak** jeongjeom
Rainbow mujigae
Cloud guleum
Lightning beongae / **Thunder** cheon-dung / **Rain** bi
Snow nun / **Ice** eol-eum / **Hail** woo-bag
Fog angae
Wind balam / **Air** gong-gi
Dawn saebyeog / **Dew** iseul
Sunset ilmol / **Sunrise** haedod-i

There is a rainbow above the waterfall.
pogpo wieneun mujigaega itseubnida.
The ocean is bigger than the sea.
daeyangneun badaboda deo keuda.
From the mountain, I can see the river.
san-eseo gang-i boibnida.
Today we hope to see snow.
oneul ulineun nun-eul bogileul huimanghabnida.
There aren't any clouds in the sky.
haneul-eneun guleum-i hanado eobs-seubnida.
I see the lightning from my window.
naneun changmun-eseo beongaeleul bonda.
I can hear the thunder from outside.
bakk-eseo cheondungsoliga deullibnida.
I want to see the sunset from the hill.
naneun eondeog-eseo ilmol-eul bogo sipda.
The lake has a shallow part and a deep part.
hosueneun yat-eun bubungwa gip-eun bubun-i itseubnida.
I don't like the wind.
naneun balam-eul joh-ahaji anhneunda.
The air on the mountain is very clear.
san-ui gong-gineun maeu malgseubnida.
Every dawn, there is dew on the leaves of my plants.
saebyeogmada nae sigmul-ui ipsagwie iteul-i maejhibnida.
Is this ice or hail?
igeos-eun eol-eum-inga ubag-inga?
I can see the volcano.
hwasan-i boineyo.
I want to climb to the summit of Hanla mountain.
hanlasan jeongsang-e oleugo sipda.

Sky haneul
World segye / **Earth** jigu / **Sun** hae
Moon dal / **Crescent** choseungdal / **Full moon** boleumdal
Star byeol / **Planet** haengseong
Fire bul / **Heat** yeol
Humidity seubgi
Agriculture nong-eob
Island seom
Cave dong-gul
Public park gong-won / **National park** guglib gong-won
Rock bawi / **Stone** dol
Ground ttang / **soil** heulg
Sea shore bada haean / **Seashell** jogae
Horizon supyeongseon / **Ray** seon
Dry maleun / **Wet** jeoj-eun
Deep gip-eun / **Shallow** yat-eun
Weeds jabcho
A stick magdaegi
Dust meonji

The moon and the stars are beautiful in the night sky.
bamhaneul-e dalgwa byeol-i cham aleumdabneyo.
The earth is a planet.
jiguneun haengseong-ida.
The heat today is unbearable.
oneul deowineun cham-eul su eobs-eul jeongdoibnida.
At the beach there is fresh air.
haebyeon-eneun sinseonhan gong-giga itseubnida.
I want to sail to the island to see the sunrise.
naneun ilchul-eul bogi wihae geu seom-eulo hanghaehago sipda.
Parts of the cave are dry and other parts are wet.
dong-gul-ui ilbuneun geonjohago daleun ilbuneun jeoj-eo itseubnida.
We live in a beautiful world.
ulineun aleumdaun sesang-e salgo itseubnida.
There is dust from the fire in the park.
gong-won-e hwajaelo inhan meonjiga itseubnida.
I want to collect seashells from the seashore.
badatga-eseo jogaekkeobdegileul mo-eugo sip-eoyo.
There are too many stones in the soil so it's impossible to use this area for agricultural purposes.
heulg-e dol-i neomu manh-a nong-gyeongjilo hwal-yonghaneun geos-eun bulganeunghada.
Why are there so many weeds growing by the swamp?
neupjidaeeneun wae ileohge jabchoga manh-i jalaneun geolkkayo?

Animals – dongmul

Pet aewan dongmul
Mammals poyulyu
Dog gae(gang-a-ji) / **Cat** goyang-i
Parrot aengmusae
Pigeon bidulgi
Pig dwaeji / **Sheep** yang
Cow amso / **Bull** hwangso
Donkey dangnagwi / **Horse** mal / **Camel** nagta
Rodent seolchilyu
Mouse saengjwi / **Rat** jwi
Rabbit tokki
Hamster haemseuteo
Duck oli / **Goose** geowi
Turkey chilmyeonjo
Chicken dalg
Poultry gageumlyu
Squirrel dalamjwi

I have a dog and two cats.
naneun gae han maliwa goyang-i du malileul kiugo itseubnida.
There is a bird on the tree.
namue saega it-eoyo.
I want to go to the zoo to see the animals.
dongmul-won-e gaseo dongmuldeul-eul bogo sip-eoyo.
My daughter wants a pet horse.
nae ttal-eun aewan-yong mal-eul wonhaeyo.
A pig, a sheep, a donkey, and a cow are considered farm animals.
dwaeji, yang, dangnagwi, soneun nongjang dongmullo ganjudoebnida.
I want a hamster as a pet.
naneun haemseuteoleul aewandongmullo kiugo sipseubnida.
A camel is a desert animal.
nagtaneun samag dongmul-ida.
Can I put ducks, geese, and turkeys inside my coop?
uli an-e oli, geowi, chilmyeonjoleul neoh-eodo doenayo?
We have rabbits and squirrels in our yard.
uli jib madang-eneun tokkiwa dalamjwiga it-eoyo.
It's cruel to keep a parrot inside a cage.
aengmusaeleul saejang an-e gaduneun geos-eun jan-inhan il-ibnida.
There are many pigeons in the city.
dosieneun bidulgiga manhseubnida.
Mice and rats are rodents.
saengjwiwa jwineun seolchilyuibnida.

Tiger holang-i
Lion saja / **Hyena** haiena
Leopard pyobeom / **Panther** pyobeom / **Cheetah** chita
Elephant kokkili / **Rhinoceros** koppulso / **Hippopotamus** - hama
Bat bagjwi
Fox yeou / **Wolf** neugdae
Weasel jogjebi
Bear gom
Deer saseum
Monkey wonsung-i
Otter sudal
Marsupial yudaemog dongmul

There are a lot of animals in the forest.
sup-eneun manh-eun dongmuldeul-i itseubnida.
The most dangerous animal in Africa is not the lion, it's the hippopotamus.
apeulika-eseo gajang wiheomhan dongmul-eun sajaga anila hamaibnida.
A wolf is much bigger than a fox.
neugdaeneun yeouboda hwolssin keubnida.
Are there bears in this forest?
i sup-e gom-i itnayo?
Bats are the only mammals that can fly.
bagjwineun nal su itneun yuilhan poyulyuida.
It's usually very difficult to see a leopard in the wild.
ilbanjeog-eulo yasaeng-eseo pyobeom-eul boneun geos-eun maeu eolyeobseubnida.
Cheetahs are common in certain regions of Africa and rare in others.
chitaneun apeulikaui teugjeong jiyeog-eseoneun heunhajiman daleun jiyeog-eseoneun deumubnida.
Elephants and rhinoceroses are known as very aggressive animals.
kokkiliwa koppulsoneun maeu gong-gyeogjeog-in dongmullo allyeojyeo itseubnida.
I saw a hyena and a panther at the safari yesterday.
eoje sapalieseo haienawa pyobeom-eul bwass-eoyo.
The largest member of the cat family is the tiger.
goyang-igwaui gajang keun guseong-won-eun holang-iibnida.
Deer hunting is forbidden in the national park.
guglibgong-won-eseoneun saseum sanyang-i geumjidoeeo isteubnida.
There are many monkeys on the branches of the trees.
namu gajieneun wonsung-iga manh-i itseubnida.
An opossum isn't a rat but it's a marsupial just like the kangaroo.
jumeonijwineun jwineun anijiman kaeng-geoluwa machangajilo yudaelyu dongmul-ibnida.

Bird sae
Crow kkamagwi
Stork hwangsae
Vulture dogsuli/**Eagle** dogsuli
Owl olppaemi
Peacock gongjag
Reptile pachung-ryu
Turtle geobug-i
Snake baem
Lizard domabaem
Crocodile ag-eo
Frog gaeguli
Seal badapyobum
Whale golae /**Dolphin** dolgolae
Fish mulgogi
Shark sang-eo
Wing nalgae /**Feather** gisteol
Tail kkoli /**Fur** teol /**Scales** bineul
Fins jineuleomi /**Horns** bbul/**Claws** jibgebal

An eagle and an owl are birds of prey however vultures are scavengers.
dogsuliwa olppaemineun maeng-geumlyuijiman dogsulineun cheongsobu-ibnida.
Crows are very smart.
kkamagwineun maeu ttogttoghabnida.
I want to see the stork migration in Europe.
yuleob-ui hwangsae idong-eul bogo sipseubnida.
Don't buy a fur coat!
mopi koteuleul saji maseyo!
Butterflies and peacocks are colorful.
nabiwa gongjagsaega dachaelobseubnida.
Some snakes are poisonous.
ilbu baem-eun yudogseong-ibnida.
Is that the sound of a cricket or a frog?
gwittulami soliingayo, gaeguli soliingayo?
Lizards, crocodiles, and turtles belong to the reptile family.
domabaem, ag-eo, geobug-ineun pachunglyugwa-e soghabnida.
I want to see the fish in the lake.
hosue saneun mulgogileul bogo sip-eoyo.
There were a lot of seals basking on the beach last week.
jinanjueneun haebyeon-e manh-eun mulgaedeul-i ilgwang-yog-eul hago it-eotseubnida.
A whale is not a fish.
golaeneun mulgogiga anibnida.

Religion - jong-gyo Holidays hyuil Traditions / customs
jeontong/gwanseub

God hananim / **Bible** seong-gyeong
Old Testament guyag seongseo / **New Testament** sin-yag seongseo
Garden of Eden eden dongsan / **Heaven** cheongug
Adam adam / **Eve** ibeu / **Angels** cheonsa / **Priest** seongjigja
Noah noa / **Ark** bangju / **Moses** mose
To pray gidohada / **Prayer** gido / **Holy** geolughan / **Faith** mid-eum
Blessing chugbog / **To bless** chugboghada
Prophet yeeonja / **Messiah** guseju / **Miracle** gijeog
Ten commandments sibgyemyeong
The five books of Moses mose-ui daseos gwon-ui chaeg
Genesis changsegi
Exodus idong / **Leviticus** lewigi / **Deuteronomy** sinmyeong-gi

What is your religion?
dangsin-ui jong-gyoneun mueos-ibnikka?
We have faith in miracles.
ulineun gijeog-eul midseubnida.
When do I need to say the blessing?
eonje chugbog-eul malhaeya habnikka?
I must say a prayer for the holiday.
myeongjeol-eul maj-a gidoleul deulyeoyagetseubnida.
The angels came from heaven.
cheonsadeul-eun haneul-eseo watseubnida.
Aaron, the brother of Moses, was the first priest.
mose-ui hyeong alon-eun cheos beonjjae jesajang-ieotseubnida.
The story of Noah's Ark and the flood is very interesting.
noaui bangjuwa hongsu iyagineun maeu heungmilobseubnida.
Adam and Eve were the first humans and they lived in the Garden of Eden.
adamgwa ibeuneun choechoui ingan-ieotgo geudeul-eun edendongsan-eseo sal-atseubnida.
Moses had to climb up on Mount Sinai to receive the Ten Commandments from God.
moseneun hananimkke sibgyemyeong-eul badgi wihae sinaesan-e ollaya haessseubnida.
The Five Books of the Moses are Genesis, Exodus, Leviticus, Numbers, and Deuteronomy.
mose-ui daseos gwon-ui chaeg-eun changsegi, chul-aegubgi, lewigi, minsugi, sinmyeong-giibnida.

Christian Religion gidoggyo jong-gyo
Church gyohoe / **Cathedral** seongdang
Catholic gatollig / **Christian** sinja
Christianity gidoggyo / **Catholicism** katolliggyo
Jesus yesu / **A cross** sibjaga
Priest seongjigja / **Holy** geolughan / **Holy** water seongsu
To sin joeleul jisda / **A sin** joe
Monastery sudowon / **Nun** sunyeo / **Chapel** yebaedang
Christmas keuliseumaseu / **Christmas eve** keuliseumaseu ibeu
Christmas tree keuliseumaseu teuli
New Year saehae / **Merry Christmas** meli keuliseumaseu
Easter buhwaljeol
Saint seongin

The church is open today.
oneul gyohoeneun yeollyeoitseubnida.
Christians love to celebrate Christmas.
geuliseudoindeul-eun keuliseumaseuleul chughahaneun geos-eul joh-ahabnida.
I need to turn on the lights on my Christmas tree for Christmas Eve.
keuliseumaseu ibeueneun keuliseumaseu teulie bul-eul kyeoya haeyo.
Two more weeks until Easter.
buhwaljeolkkaji ap-eulo 2ju nam-atseubnida.
The nuns live in the monastery.
sunyeodeul-eun sudowon-e sanda.
The priest read a psalm from the Bible in front of the congregation.
sinbuneun hoejung ap-eseo seong-gyeong-ui sipyeon-eul nangdoghaetseubnida.
I went to pray in the cathedral.
naneun daeseongdang-e gidohaleo gatda.
Jesus is the son of God.
yesunim-eun hananim-ui adeul-ibnida.
I have a gold necklace with a cross.
naneun sibjagaga dallin geum moggeol-ileul gajigo itseubnida.
Merry Christmas and Happy New Year to all my friends and family.
modeun chinguwa gajogdeul-ege jeulgeoun keuliseumaseuwa saehae bog manh-i bad-euseyo.
Peter is a famous saint in Christianity.
bedeuloneun gidoggyoeseo yumyeonghan seong-in-ida.
The priest baptized the baby in the holy water.
sinbuneun agiege seongsulo selyeleul jueotda.
The devil and the demons are from hell.
magwiwa gwisin-eun jiog-eseo watseubnida.
Many schools refuse to teach evolution.
manh-eun haggyoeseo jinhwalon-eul galeuchigileul geobuhabnida.

Jew yutaein
Judaism yutaegyo
Religious jong-gyoui
Monotheism ilsingyo
Synagogue yutae gyohoedang
Kosher kosher
Passover yuwoljeol
Menorah menola
Dreidel deuleidel
Goblet gobeullis
Wine wain
Circumcision hallye
Islam iseullam
Muslim museulim
Mosque sawon
Hindu hindu
Buddhist bulgyo in
Temple jeol

The Jews worship at the synagogue.
yudaeindeul-eun hoedang-eseo yebaeleul deulibnida.
The Bible is a holy book which tells the story of the Jewish nations and includes many miracles.
seong-gyeong-eun yudae minjog-ui iyagileul damgo it-eumyeo manh-eun gijeog-eul damgo itneun geolughan chaeg-ibnida.
In Judaism, they pray three times a day. Morning prayer, afternoon prayer, and evening prayer.
yudaegyoeseoneun halue se beonssig gidohabnida. achimgido, ohugido, jeonyeoggidoibnida.
The three forefathers are Abraham, Isaac, and Jacob.
se josang-eun abeulaham, isag, yagob-ibnida.
To learn about the Holocaust and the concentration camps is very important.
hollokoseuteuwa gangje suyongso-e daehae baeuneun geos-eun maeu jung-yohabnida.
The monotheistic faiths use the bible.
yuilsingyoneun seong-gyeong-eul sayonghabnida.
Muslims pray at the mosque.
museullimdeul-eun moseukeueseo gidohanda.
In Islam they must pray five times a day.
iseullam-eseoneun halue daseos beonssig gidohaeya habnida.

Wedding and Relationship - gyeolhonsiggwa gwangye

Wedding gyeolhonsig
Wedding hall gyeolhonsig jang
Married gihon
Civil wedding jiyeog gyeolhonsig
Bride sinbu
Groom sinlang
Ceremony uisig
Reception lisebsyeon
Chapel yebaedang
Engagement yaghon
Engagement ring yaghon banji
Wedding ring gyeolhon banji
Anniversary ginyeom-il
Honeymoon sinhon yeohaeng
Fiancé yaghonja
Husband nampyeon
Wife bu-in

When is the wedding?
gyeolhonsig-eun eonjeibnikka?
We are having the service in the chapel and the reception in the wedding hall.
yebaeneun yebaedang-eseo, piloyeon-eun yesigjang-eseo jinhaenghago itseubnida.
Our anniversary is on Valentine's Day.
uli ginyeom-il-eun ballentaindeiyeyo.
This is my engagement ring and this is my wedding ring.
igeos-eun nae yaghonbanjiigo igeos-eun nae gyeolhonbanjiibnida.
They are finally married so now it's time for the honeymoon.
deudieo gyeolhon-eul haet-euni ije sinhon-yeohaeng-eul tteonal sigan-ida.
He decided to propose to his girlfriend. She said "yes" and now they are engaged.
geuneun yeojachinguege peulopojeuhagilo gyeoljeonghaetda. geunyeoneun "ye"lago malhaeygo ije geudeul-eun yaghonhaetda.
He is my fiancé now. Next year he will be my husband.
geuneun ije nae yaghonjaida. naenyeon-e geuneun nae nampyeon-i doel geos-ida.
Three civil weddings are taking place at the courthouse today.
oneul beob-won-eseoneun se beon-ui jiyeog gyeolhonsig-i geohaengdoebnida.
The bride and groom received many presents.
sinlangsinbuneun manh-eun seonmul-eul bad-astseubnida

Valentine day ballentain dei
Love salang
To love salanghada
In love salang-e ppajin
Romantic lomaentig
Darling yeobo
A date daeiteu
A relationship gwangye
Boyfriend namja chingu
Girlfriend yeoja chingu
To hug kkyeoanda
A hug poong
To kiss kiseuhada
A kiss kiseu
Single mihon
Divorced ihon
Widow gwabu

I am in love with her.
naneun geunyeowa salang-e ppajyeotseubnida.
I am in love with him.
naneun geuwa salang-e ppajyeotseubnida.
I love her (male to female).
naneun geunyeoleul salanghabnida.
I love him (female to male).
naneun geuleul salanghabnida.
I love you.
salanghaeyo.
You are very romantic.
dangsin-eun maeu nangmanjeog-ibnida.
They have a very good relationship.
geudeul-eun maeu joh-eun gwangyeleul gajigo itseubnida.
The husband and wife are in a relationship.
nampyeongwa anaeneun gwangyeleul maejgo itseubnida.
I am single because I divorced my wife.
jeoneun anaewa ihonhaetgi ttaemun-e mihon-ibnida.
She is my darling and my love.
geunyeoneun naui yeoja chingu-ija salang-ibnida.
I want to kiss you and hug you in this picture.
naneun i sajin sog-e dangsin-ege kiseuhago sipgo poonghago sipseubnida

Politics – jeongchi

Flag gug-gi
National anthem gugga
Nation gugga(nala)
National guggaui
International gugjejeog-in
Local hyeonji
Patriot aegugja
Symbol sangjing
Peace pyeonghwa
Treaty joyag
State do
Country nala
County gun
Century segi
Majority dasu
Local hyeonji
Campaign undong
Annexation buga
Startegic jeonlyagjeog
Plan gyehoeg
Decision gyeoljeong

This is a political movement which is supported by the majority.
ineun dasuui jijileul badneun jeongchijeog undong-ida.
This flag is the national symbol of the country.
i guggineun geu nalaui guggaleul sangjinghanda.
This is all politics.
igeos-eun modu jeongchiibnida.
There is a difference between state law and local law.
jubeobgwa jibangbeob-eneun chaiga itseubnida.
He is a patriot of the nation.
geuneun minjog-ui aegugjaida.
Most countries have a national anthem.
daebubun-ui nala-eneun gugga(gugga)ga itseubnida.
This is a political campaign to demand independence.
igeos-eun doglib-eul yoguhaneun jeongchijeog kaempein-ibnida.
The annexation plan was a strategic decision.
habbyeong gyehoeg-eun jeonlyagjeog gyeoljeong-ieotseubnida.

Law beob
Illegal bulbeob / **Legal** habbeob
International law gugjebeob
Human rights ingwon
Punishment cheobeol / **Torture** gomun
Execution (to kill) cheohyeong
Spy seupai
Amnesty teugsa / **Political asylum** jeongchijeog mangmyeong
Republic gonghwagug
Dictator dogjaeja
Citizen simin
Resident geojuja
Immigrant imin
Public gong-gong / **Private** sajeog
Racism injong chabyul
Government jeongbu
Revolution hyeogmyeong
Civilian mingan-in
Population ingu
Socialism sahoejuui / **Communism** gongsanjuui

There were many protests and riots today.
oneul-eun manh-eun siwiwa pogdong-i it-eotseubnida.
The civilian population wanted a revolution.
mingan-indeul-eun hyeogmyeong-eul wonhaetseubnida.
The politicians want to ask the president to give the captured spy amnesty.
jeongchiindeul-eun chepodoen gancheob-eul samyeonhae dallago daetonglyeong-ege ganchunghago sip-eohanda.
Although he was the brutal dictator of the republic, in private he was a nice person.
bilog geuneun gonghwagug-ui janhoghan dogjaejayeotjiman, gaeinjeog-euloneun joh-eun salam-ieotseubnida.
In some countries torture and execution is a common form of legitimate punishment.
ilbu gugga-eseoneun gomungwa cheohyeong-i habbeobjeog-in cheobeol-ui ilbanjeog-in hyeongtaeibnida.
This is a violation of human rights and international law.
ineun ingwongwa gugjebeob-eul wibanhaneun haeng-wiibnida.
Communism and socialism were popular in the 19th century.
19segieneun gongsanjuuiwa sahoejuuiga yuhaenghaetda.
In which county is this legal?
eoneu kauntieseo igeos-i habbeobjeog-ingayo?

President daetonglyeong
Statement seongmyeong
Presidential daetonglyeong
Vice president butonglyeong
Defense minister gugbangjang-gwan
Interior minister naemu jang-gwan
Exterior minister oemujang-gwan
Prime minister chongli
Election seongeo
Poll tupyo
Campaign undong
Candidate huboja
Democracy minjujuui
Movement umjig-im
Politician jeongchiga
Politics jeongchi
To vote tupyohada
Majority dasu
Independence doglib
Party pati
Veto geobugwon
Impeachment goso
Convoy hosong

They want to appoint him as defense minister.
geudeul-eun geuleul gugbangjang-gwan-eulo immyeonghago sip-eohabnida.
Both parties want to veto the impeachment inquiry.
yangdang modu tanhaeg josaleul geobuhago sip-eohanda.
I want to see the presidential convoy.
daetonglyeong hosongchalyang-eul bogo sipseubnida.
In some countries other than the United States, they have a prime minister, interior minister, and exterior minister.
migug ioeui ilbu gugga-eneun chongli, naemujang-gwan, oemujang-gwan-i itseubnida.
I want to meet the president and the vice president.
daetonglyeong-gwa butonglyeong-eul mannago sipseubnida.
I want to go to the election polls to vote for the new candidate.
sae hubo-ege tupyohagi wihae seongeo tupyoso-e gago sipseubnida.
We support democracy and are against fascism and racism.
ulineun minjujuuileul jijihamyeo pasijeumgwa injongchabyeoljuuie bandaehabnida.

United Nations yuen(guk-je yonhab)
Condemnation binan
United States migug
European Union yuleob yeonhab
Coup kudeta
Treason ban-yeog
Fascism pasijeum
Resistance jeohang / **Rebels** banyeog-ja
Members hoewon
Captured salojaphim / **To capture** salojaphida
Ambassador daesa
Embassy daesagwan / **Consulate** yeongsagwan
Biased pyun-hyang
Unilateral ilbangjeog
Bilateral yangchog
Resolution haegyeol
Sanctions jejae

All the members of the resistance were accused of treason and had to ask for political asylum.
jeohangselyeog-eun modu ban-yeogjoelo gisodoeeo jeongchijeog mangmyeong-eul yocheonghaeya haetseubnida.
The resolution is biased.
Haegyeol-e pyeonhyangdoeeo itseubnida.
This was an official condemnation.
ineun gongsigjeog-in binan-ieotseubnida.
The United Nations is located in New York.
yuen-eun nyuyog-e wichihae itseubnida.
I am a United States citizen and a resident of the European Union.
jeoneun migug simin-ija yuleob-yeonhab geojujaibnida.
This is the ambassador's residence is located near the embassy.
igos-eun daesagwan geuncheoe wichihan daesagwanjeoibnida.
I need the phone number and address of the consulate.
yeongsagwan jeonhwabeonhowa jusoga pil-yohaeyo.
Are consular services available today?
oneul yeongsa seobiseuga ganeunghabnikka?
The international peace treaty needs to include both sides.
gugjepyeonghwajoyag-eneun yangcheug moduga pohamdoeeoya habnida.
According to the government, the rebels carried out an illegal coup.
jeongbue ttaleumyeon bangun-eun bulbeob kudetaleul gamhaenghaetda.
They must impose sanctions against that country.
geu nala-e daehae jejaeleul gahaeya habnida.

Military – gundae

Army gundae / **Armed forces** gundae
Navy haegun / **Soldier** gunin / **Troops** gun-in, gundae
A force budae / **Ground forces** jisang-gun
Base beiseu / **Headquarter** bonsa / **Intelligence** gimil yowon
Ranks sun-wi
Sergeant jungsa / **Lieutenant** jungwee
The general jang-gun / **Commander** salyeong-gwan
Colonel daelyeong / **Military chief of Staff** gunchammochongjang
Enlistment ibdae / **Reserves** yebigun / **War** jeonjaeng
Terrorism teleo / **Terrorist** teleoliseuteu / **Insurgency** banlan
Border crossing guggyeong tong-gwa
Refugee nanmin / **Camp** kaempeu

I want to enlist in the military.
naneun gundaee ibdaehago sipda.
This base is designated for military aircrafts only.
i gijineun gun-yong hang-gong-gi jeon-yong-eulo jijeongdoeeotseubnida.
That is the headquarters of the enemy.
geugos-eun jeog-ui bonbu-ibnida.
This country has a powerful airforce.
i nala-eneun ganglyeoghan gong-gun-i itseubnida.
They need to enlist reserve forces for the war.
geudeul-eun jeonjaeng-eul wihae yebigun-eul mojibhaeya habnida.
Welcome to the border crossing.
guggyeong tong-gwa-e osin geos-eul hwan-yeonghabnida.
Military intelligence relies on important sources of information.
gunsa jeongboneun jung-yohan jeongbo soseue uijonhabnida.
The military chief of staff was the target of a failed assassination attempt.
gun chammochongjang-eun silpaehan amsal sidoui pyojeog-ieotda.
The sniper killed the highest-ranking lieutenant.
jeogyeogsuneun choegowi jung-wileul jug-yeotseubnida.
The terrorist group claimed responsibility for the car-bomb attack at the refugee camp.
teleo dancheneun nanmin kaempeueseo balsaenghan chalyang pogtan gong-gyeog-i jasindeul-ui sohaeng-ilago jujanghaetseubnida.
It's impossible to defeat terrorism because it's an ideology.
teleolijeum-eul mullichineun geos-eun inyeom-igi ttaemun-e bulganeunghabnida.
Several of the submarine sailors were missing in action.
jamsuham seon-won jung myeotmyeog-i siljongdoeeotseubnida.

Airstrike gongseub / **Air force** gong-gun
Fighter jet jeontugi / **Military aircraft** gun-yong hang-gong-gi
Drone mu-in bihaeng-gi (dron)
Stealth technology seutelseu gisul
Tank taengkeu / **Submarine** jamsuham / **Weapon** mugi / **Bullet** chong-al
Grenade sulyutan / **Mine** gaeng / **Bomb** pogtan / **Explosion** pogbal
Sniper jeogyeogbyeong / **Gun** chong / **Rifle** sochong
Missile misail / **Mortar** baggyeogpo
Anti tank missile daejeoncha misail / **Anti aircraft missile** daegongmisail
Shoulder fire missile shoulder fire misail
Ammunition tan-yag / **Artillery** po / **Artillery shell** potan
Precision missile jeongmilmisail / **Ballistic missile** tando misail
Atomic bomb wonja pogtan / **Nuclear weapon** haegmugi
Weapon of mass destruction daelyangsalsangmugi
Chemical weapon hwahag mugi
Flare system peulleeo siseutem
Supply gong-geub / **Storage** jeojang

The M-16 is a US-made rifle.
M-16eun migugsan sochong-ida.
The tank fired artillery shells.
taengkeuneun potan-eul balsahaetseubnida.
Shoulder-fired missiles are extremely dangerous and are hard to defend against.
Shoulder-fired misail-eun maeu wiheomhamyeo bang-eohagi eolyeobseubnida. **The flare system is meant as a defense against anti-aircraft missiles.**
peulleeo siseutem-eun daegong misail-e daehan bang-eoleul uimihabnida.
The navy was able to intercept a missile.
haegun-eun misail-eul yogyeoghal su it-eotda.
At the terrorist safe-house, guns, bullets, and grenades were found.
teleoliseuteu eunsincheoeseoneun chong, chong-al, sulyutan-i balgyeondwaetda.
The coalition forces struck an enemy arms depot.
yeonhabgun-eun jeog-ui mugi chang-goleul gong-gyeoghaetseubnida.
An intense missile attack was carried out against the supply forces that resulted in many casualties.
bogeubgun-e daehae ganglyeoghan misail gong-gyeog-i silsidoeeo manh-eun sasangjaga balsaenghaetseubnida.
The terrorist cell fired ballistic missiles at the nuclear facility site.
teleojojig-eun haegsiseol bujie tandomisail-eul balsahaetda.
Atomic bombs and chemical weapons are weapons of mass destruction.
wonjapogtangwa hwahagmugineun daelyangsalsangmugiida.

A target pyojeog / **To target** tages-eulo samda
An attack gong-gyeog / **To attack** gong-gyeoghada
To shoot ssoda / **To open** fire bul-eul piuda
Intense - ganglyeolham/ **Fired** haegodoem
Assassination amsal / **Assassin** amsalja / **Enemy** jeog
Reconnaissance jeongchal / **To infiltrate** chimtuhada
Exchange of fire gyojeon / **A cease fire** hyujeon
Withdrawal cheolsu / **Invasion** chim-ib
To defeat paebaehada / **To surrender** tuhanghada
Victim pihaeja / **Injury** busang / **Deaths** samangja / **To kill** jug-ida
Prisoner of war jeonjaeng polo / **Missing in action** siljong
Act of war jeonjaeng haeng-wi / **War crimes** jeonjaeng beomjoe
Defense bang-eo / **Attempt** sido

There is an invasion of ground forces.
jisang-gun-ui chimgong-i itseubnida.
The soldier wanted to open fire and shoot at the invading forces.
gun-in-eun chimlyaggun-ege chong-gyeog-eul gahago chong-gyeog-eul gahago sip-eotseubnida.
The bomb attack was considered an act of aggression and an act of war.
pogtan gong-gyeog-eun chimlyag haeng-wiija jeonjaeng haeng-wilo ganjudoeeotseubnida.
The reconnaissance drone managed to infiltrate deep within enemy territory.
jeongchal deulon-eun jeog yeongto gipsug-i chimtuhaneun de seong-gonghaetseubnida.
The airstrike targeted an ammunition storage site.
gongseub-eun tan-yag jeojang-goleul mogpyolo sam-atseubnida.
The mortar attack and exchange of fire caused injuries and deaths on both sides.
baggyeogpo gong-gyeoggwa chong-gyeogjeon-eulo yangcheug modu busang-gwa samang-i balsaenghaetseubnida.
First, we need to clear the mines.
meonjeo jiloeleul jegeohaeya habnida.
The ceasefire agreement included the release of prisoners of war.
hyujeonhyeobjeong-eneun jeonjaengpolo seogbangdo pohamdwaetda.
The army made a public statement to announce the withdrawal.
gun-eun gong-gae seongmyeong-eul tonghae cheolsuleul seon-eonhaetda.
There was a huge explosion as a result of the terrorist attack.
teleo gong-gyeog-eulo inhae eomcheongnan pogbal-i il-eonatseubnida.
The commander of the insurgency was accused of serious war crimes.
banlangun salyeong-gwan-eun mugeo-un jeonjaeng beomjoe hyeom-uilo gisodoeeotseubnida.

Conclusion

Hopefully, you have enjoyed this book and will use the knowledge you have learned in various situations in your everyday life. In contrast to other methods of learning foreign languages, the theory in this current usage is that ever-greater topics can be broached so that one's vocabulary can expand. This method relies on the discovery I made of the list of core words from each language. Once these are learned, your conversational learning skills will progress very quickly.

You are now ready to discuss sport and school and office-related topics and this will open up your world to a more satisfying extent. Humans are social creatures and language helps us interact. Indeed, at times, it can keep us alive, such as in war situations. You might find yourself in dangerous situations perhaps as a journalist, military personnel or civilian and you need to be armed with the appropriate vocabulary.

"This is a base for military aircraft only," you may have to tell some people who try to enter a field you are protecting, or know what you are being told when someone says to you, "Welcome to the border crossing." As a journalist on a foreign assignment, you may need to quickly understand what you are being told, such as "The sniper killed the highest-ranking lieutenant." If you are someone negotiating on behalf of the army, you may need to find another lieutenant very quickly. Lives, at times, literally depend on your level of understanding and comprehension.

This unique approach that I first discovered when using this method to learn on my own, will have helped you speak the Korean language much quicker than any other way.

Congratulations! Now You Are on Your Own!

If you merely absorb the required words in this book, you will then have acquired the basis to become conversational in Korean! After memorizing these words, this conversational foundational basis that you have just gained will trigger your ability to make improvements in conversational fluency at an amazing speed! However, in order to engage in quick and easy conversational communication, you need a special type of basics, and this book will provide you with just that.

Unlike the foreign language learning systems presently used in schools and universities, along with books and programs that are available on the market today, that focus on *everything* but being conversational, *this* method's sole focus is on becoming conversational in Korean as well as any other language. Once you have successfully mastered the required words in this book, there are two techniques that if combined with these essential words, can further enhance your skills and will result in you improving your proficiency tenfold. *However*, these two techniques will only succeed *if* you have completely and successfully absorbed these required words. *After* you establish the basis for fluent communications by memorizing these words, you can enhance your conversational abilities even more if you use the following two techniques.

The first step is to attend a Korean language class that will enable you to sharpen your grammar. You will gain additional vocabulary and learn past and present tenses, and if you apply these skills that you learn in the class, together with these words that you have previously memorized, you will be improving your conversational skills tenfold. You will notice that, conversationally, you will succeed at a much higher rate than any of your classmates. A simple second technique is to choose Korean subtitles while watching a movie. If you have successfully mastered and grasped these words, then the combination of the two—those words along with the subtitles—will aid you considerably in putting all the grammar into perspective, and again, conversationally, you will improve tenfold.

Once you have established a basis of quick and easy conversation in Korean with those words that you just attained, every additional word or grammar rule you pick up from there on will be gravy. And these additional words or grammar rules can be combined with the these words, enriching your conversational abilities even more. Basically, after the research and studies I've conducted with my method over the years, I came to the conclusion that in order to become conversational, you first must learn the words and *then* learn the grammar.

NOTE FROM THE AUTHOR

Thank you for your interest in my work. I encourage you to share your overall experience of this book by posting a review. Your review can make a difference! Please feel free to describe how you benefited from my method or provide creative feedback on how I can improve this program. I am constantly seeking ways to enhance the quality of this product, based on personal testimonials and suggestions from individuals like you.

Thanks and best of luck,
Yatir Nitzany

Also by Yatir Nitzany

Conversational Spanish Quick and Easy

Conversational French Quick and Easy

Conversational Italian Quick and Easy

Conversational Portuguese Quick and Easy

Conversational German Quick and Easy

Conversational Dutch Quick and Easy

Conversational Norwegian Quick and Easy

Conversational Danish Quick and Easy

Conversational Swedish Quick and Easy

Conversational Finnish Quick and Easy

Conversational Russian Quick and Easy

Conversational Ukrainian Quick and Easy

Conversational Bulgarian Quick and Easy

Conversational Polish Quick and Easy

Conversational Hebrew Quick and Easy

Conversational Yiddish Quick and Easy

Conversational Armenian Quick and Easy

Conversational Romanian Quick and Easy

Conversational Arabic Quick and Easy

www.ingramcontent.com/pod-product-compliance
Lightning Source LLC
Chambersburg PA
CBHW070147080526
44586CB00015B/1881